CLAYTON LECTURES

Power and Diplomacy
Dean Acheson (1957–1958)

Diplomacy in the Nuclear Age
Lester B. Pearson (1958–1959)

The Diplomacy of Economic Development
Eugene R. Black (1959–1960)

European Economic Integration and the Western Alliance
Paul-Henri Spaak (1960–1961)

United Europe: Challenge and Opportunity
Walter Hallstein (1961–1962)

THE FLETCHER SCHOOL OF LAW AND DIPLOMACY

A Graduate School of International Affairs
Administered with the Cooperation of Harvard University

TUFTS UNIVERSITY | MEDFORD, MASSACHUSETTS

UNITED EUROPE
Challenge and Opportunity

The William L. Clayton Lectures on International
Economic Affairs and Foreign Policy

UNITED EUROPE

Challenge and Opportunity

WALTER HALLSTEIN

HARVARD UNIVERSITY PRESS

Cambridge, Massachusetts | 1962

THE WILLIAM L. CLAYTON LECTURES

The William L. Clayton Center for International Economic Affairs was established in 1952 at the Fletcher School of Law and Diplomacy, Tufts University, in honor and recognition of Mr. Clayton's services as one of the country's leading business-statesmen and its first Under Secretary of State for Economic Affairs. Mr. Clayton is founder and retired head of Anderson, Clayton & Company, the world's largest cotton merchants. His public service includes the following offices: Assistant Secretary of Commerce, 1942–44; Administrator of the Surplus War Property Administration; Assistant Secretary of State, 1944–46; and Under Secretary of State for Economic Affairs, 1946–48.

The foundation of the William L. Clayton Center was officially sponsored by the American Cotton Shippers Association, honoring "the accomplishments of Mr. Clayton both in the international cotton trade and as a public servant in the field of economic diplomacy," and "as a means of recognizing his substantial service to the Nation and extending the influence of his example in the field of international trade and diplomacy." Some two hundred individuals, business firms, banks, and foundations—principally connected with the cotton trade—joined in contributing the endowment for the Clayton Center.

The program of the Clayton Center—devoted to education and research—includes the William L. Clayton Professorship of International Economic Affairs, a program of research and current policy studies, a program of Clayton Fellowships to encourage and assist outstanding young men and women to prepare for careers in international economic affairs and diplomacy, and the annual Clayton Lectures by persons distinguished in the field of diplomacy, trade, or scholarship in international affairs. The Clayton Lectures were inaugurated by former Secretary of State Dean Acheson, in October 1957, which also marked the twenty-fifth year of the Fletcher School of Law and Diplomacy.

TO MY AMERICAN FRIENDS

PREFACE

The lectures which follow were given at the Fletcher
School of Law and Diplomacy, Tufts University, in
April 1962. My especial thanks are due to the Dean and
Faculty for their very kind invitation as well as for the
warm hospitality which they showed me during a visit
that for me was as memorable as it was enjoyable.

In preparing the present text for a wider public, I have
added some supplementary matter, but I have refrained
from revising the lectures themselves. The title of this
book, *United Europe: Challenge and Opportunity*, may
perhaps be regarded as an oblique reference to the trade
expansion program proposed by President Kennedy a
few months before the lectures were written; but it has a
general validity which is, I think, permanent. What I
have tried to show, indeed, in the following pages is that
all the challenges that face us in the world today are also
opportunities, and that unity in Europe—itself a firm
attempt to seize the opportunity that such challenges present—is also in turn a challenge and an opportunity for
Europeans, and for free peoples the world over. What
it means, in fact, is not the magnification of nineteenth-
century nationalism to a more than national scale, but a

chance to transform the old order of international relations and, by building anew, to build better.

It is now over twelve years since the first foundation was laid by the Declaration of M. Robert Schuman on May 9, 1950. The European Community already has a history. In the first of these lectures, I have sought to trace that history in brief. In the second, I have sketched some of the economic ideas that underlie the Community's workings, and some of the achievements to which it can so far point. Finally, I have attempted to draw out some of the political implications which this new *zōon politikon* holds for Europe, for America, and for the free world as a whole.

My present task would not be complete without one final word of thanks, not only to my American hosts, but also to those colleagues and friends in Europe whose support and encouragement have been so generously given, and above all to the peoples and statesmen whose unflagging and devoted efforts are making a united Europe, once a dream, today a reality.

Walter Hallstein

Brussels, May 1962

CONTENTS

UNITED EUROPE

Challenge and Opportunity

I THE HISTORY OF EUROPEAN INTEGRATION

ONE HUNDRED and thirty-one years ago, two young Frenchmen visited the United States in order to study the American prison system. Their report on the subject was so brilliant that it won an award from the French Academy. One of them was inspired to write a second work—not about prisons, but about freedom, the freedom that he had seen and known in the New World, although it was still far from perfect in the Old.

The young man's name was Alexis de Tocqueville, and the title of his book was *Democracy in America*. To reread it today is to be struck time and again by its astonishing insight. Living as he did in the midst of the technological revolution that was to transform the world, Tocqueville took the fact of change as his fundamental premise. He realized that it was the rapidity of change that made the modern age different in kind, not just in degree, from all the ages of the past.

Now, for the first time, man was able to exploit the riches of the earth from which his forebears had merely scratched a living—making possible a new kind of life in a society of men equal and free. Simultaneously, modern medicine was to begin its long and painful struggle against disease. But this in turn was to help bring about a vast multiplication of the world's population, millions of whom were to remain sunk in a misery worse than that of the Dark Ages in Europe. Meanwhile, the power of man's weapons of destruction was to grow in the same proportion as his mastery over nature. The golden prospect of the future was darkened by poverty and fear. What was more, the world itself was to grow relatively smaller as man's enterprise spread. Within Tocqueville's lifetime, the railways were to begin to unite continents, steamships were to begin to link them together, and the telegraph was to begin to make possible instantaneous communication over thousands of miles. In our own lifetime, these early marvels have been eclipsed by automobiles, jets, television, and space rockets. "The nations," wrote Tocqueville, "seem to be advancing to unity. Our means of intellectual intercourse unite the most remote parts of the earth; and it is impossible for men to remain strangers to each other, or to be ignorant of the events which are taking place in any corner of the globe."[1] Already, in fact, the word "foreigner" was becoming out-of-date.

By the same process, as Tocqueville saw, the already shrinking globe was becoming a world of giants. "There are at the present time," he said, "two great nations in the world which seem to tend toward the same end, although they started from different points: I allude to the Russians and the Americans. Both of them have grown up unnoticed; and while the attention of mankind was directed elsewhere, they have suddenly assumed a most prominent place among the nations; and the world learned of their existence and their greatness at almost the same time." The American nation, he continued, "gives free scope to the unguided exertions and common sense of the citizens; the Russian centres all the authority of society in a single arm: the principal instrument of the former is freedom; of the latter servitude." Each of these great powers, Tocqueville thought, "seems to be marked out . . . to sway the destinies of half of the globe."[2]

So much was clear to Tocqueville when he wrote his great treatise in 1835; yet it was more than a century before his fellow Europeans, and mankind in general, drew the political conclusions from what he had observed. In studying America, he had declared, "my wish has been to find instruction by which we may ourselves profit." "I cannot believe," he said, "that the Creator made man to leave him in an endless struggle with the . . . miseries which surround us: God destines a calmer and more certain future to the communities of Europe."[3] Yet Europe's future—and the world's—was to be far from calm. The progress of technology, the improvement of communications, the consequent drawing-together of distant peoples, and the emergence of giant powers proceeded apace. But the world's political organization lamentably failed to keep up with them. As Goethe had put it, "Mankind advances, but man remains

the same." Europe and the world both remained disunited;
and twice in a single generation, European conflicts
dragged the world into war. It was only, in fact, on the
morrow of the second world war that European statesmen began in practice to build the "calmer and more
certain future" that Tocqueville had seen as destined
for "the communities of Europe." They did so by
creating a new community, a European Community;
and they thereby set in motion a process which is already
helping to transform the international scene as a whole.

Essentially, the motives for building a European Community were the same forces that had already impressed
Tocqueville. The pressure of technology, increasing
interdependence, a growing sense that in a world of giants
nations on the old scale must band together—all these
played their part in reviving an idea of European unity
that was already of long standing. It would be superfluous to enumerate the countless political philosophers,
from Pierre Dubois in the fourteenth century to Joseph
Proudhon in the nineteenth, whose writings helped to
keep that ideal alive. A number of great names may be
cited: Maximilian Duc de Sully, friend and adviser of King
Henry IV of France; the English Quaker William Penn;
the French politician Claude Henri de Saint Simon;
the Swiss philosopher Jean Jacques Rousseau; the German
philosopher Immanuel Kant; Giuseppe Manzini, the hero
of the Italian liberation and unification movement; the
political theorist Konstantin Frantz; the French poet
Victor Hugo; and many others. But it was not until the
twentieth century that the motives for unity in Europe

became particular and pressing enough for statesmen
to act. It was not until 1919, in fact, after a European
war that had developed into the first world war, that
serious efforts were made to reform international relations. The immediate upshot of these efforts was the
League of Nations, itself in some respects a mainly European body. A few years later there came the proposals
of Aristide Briand, backed by those of Stresemann, for
what was then already called "a United States of
Europe." Behind this project lay the need to cement
unity and peace between France and Germany. But in
1930, the very year of M. Briand's memorandum, the
National Socialist party scored its first unholy victory;
and in the appalling barbarities that followed, all hope
was buried for another fifteen years.

World War I had proved the fearful destructiveness
of European quarrels fought out with modern weapons.
World War II re-emphasized that truth. Furthermore,
its aftermath publicly revealed what had already become
obvious to economic experts after World War I: that
is, that Europe's position in the world had been dras-
tically altered, partly by war itself, and partly by the
growth of those two continental giants, America and
Russia, whose importance Tocqueville had so clearly
foreseen.

In these changed circumstances, the ideal of European unity took on added strength. Throughout the war,
it had never been entirely eclipsed, either in the minds
of statesmen, or in the aspirations of refugees, Resistance
fighters, political prisoners, and ordinary men and women

throughout the continent. The study of its slow matur-
ing would make a fascinating task for some future his-
torian. His narrative, however, would have to record
the gradual disappointment of the more ambitious hopes
raised by the San Francisco Conference and embodied
in attempts to achieve unity on a wider scale, both in the
world and in Europe. Winston Churchill's speech at
Fulton, Missouri, was one of the first explicit statements
of this disappointment; but even after the so-called
"Iron Curtain" had descended and the "Cold War" was
generally acknowledged to have begun, the first practical move toward the reordering of Europe was made
in a form designed explicitly to be open to the participation of Eastern European countries. It was only when
the Soviet Union vetoed such participation that the
effort had to be confined to Western Europe.

The first decisive step was taken in 1947, with the an-
nouncement by General George Marshall of the plan for
American aid to Europe to which posterity has given
his name. The economic significance of this proposal requires no stressing: Europeans can never be oblivious of
the courage, the wisdom, and the generosity that it represented, or of the vital foundation which it laid for
European recovery. All Europe's economic "miracles"
date from then. It has to be admitted, however, that the
political results of Marshall Aid, and of the Organization for European Economic Cooperation (OEEC)
which sprang from it, fell far short of the hopes it had
originally aroused. To say this is not to decry the economic achievements of the OEEC and the European

Payments Union to which it gave birth; nor is it to belittle the ability and the efforts of those who worked so devotedly to serve them. But it is worthwhile to recall that in July 1947, when the parent Committee of Economic Cooperation met in Paris, its participants explicitly discussed the possibility of establishing, not just an international organization for cooperation in economic matters, but a full-scale European customs union which would have led inescapably, as I shall suggest later, to some form of political unity. The scope of the OEEC was much more restricted; and its structure, despite attempts to reform it, remained that of a classical intergovernmental conference in permanent session. Its executive body was a Council subject to unanimous voting; although abstention was not held to invalidate otherwise unanimous decisions, application of agreements was limited to those countries who had not abstained. Moreover, a contrary vote sufficed to veto an otherwise unanimous decision—a fact which sometimes created difficulties, even if it failed to prevent the formation of something like a general European consciousness which was to prepare the way for further steps.

If the OEEC was therefore somewhat disappointing to those of its sponsors who had hoped for real and rapid unity in Europe, the same was true of its political counterpart, the Council of Europe. This too, it should be emphasized, was not without influence as a preparation and as a training ground for more ambitious ventures. In fact, it is all too easy to forget the amount of modest but valuable work it has achieved, including the establishment of the European Convention for the Protection of Human Rights and Fundamental Freedoms, such agreements in social matters as those on Social Security and Social and Medical Assistance, and the establishment of the European Cultural Convention and the activities which have sprung from it. Nevertheless, it is against the intentions of its founders that the Council of Europe must be measured. Its remote forebear is perhaps to be found in the famous speech of Winston Churchill at the University of Zurich in September 1946, calling for "a kind of United States of Europe" (although Churchill had proposed a "Council of Europe" even earlier—in a wartime broadcast made in 1943). The immediate progenitor of the Council, however, was the Congress of Europe held in The Hague in May 1948, at which the leaders of most of the private organizations that were pressing for unity in Europe came together to call for political and economic union, a European Assembly, and a European Court. It was at this congress, incidentally, that I first met Konrad Adenauer, a man who would later play such an essential part in European integration.

When the governments of Western European countries met to consider these proposals, there was already some disagreement as to how they should be implemented; some delegations were even opposed to the whole idea of setting up an assembly of parliamentarians. The British government proposed a council of national delegations to be appointed by governments; a Franco-Belgian proposal envisaged a broad assembly whose members would be appointed by the parliaments and would vote as individuals on a majority system, the resultant resolutions being submitted to an intergovernmental council. These ideas subsequently crystallized into two separate proposals, one for a bicameral system of ministerial council and assembly, the other for a council comprising a committee of ministers and a conference of government delegates. The result was an unsatisfactory compromise which established both a Committee of Ministers, and a Consultative Assembly whose powers were extremely confined. At the beginning, indeed, the Assembly was not even allowed to fix its own agenda. Moreover, the Committee of Ministers, like that of OEEC, was bound by unanimous voting and therefore subject to veto by any single member. Despite high hopes in the Council of Europe's early sessions, therefore, and once more despite the sterling efforts of a number of dedicated Europeans, the outcome of all these strivings and deliberations was a deep sense of frustration matched by a mounting sense of urgency as the growing tensions of the Cold War made it more and more important for Western Europe to seek strength in unity.

I have dwelt upon these early ventures in European cooperation because they form the background against which it is possible to see more clearly the true significance of the movement that was about to begin. This was the movement for European integration, as distinct from mere cooperation; and its starting point was the famous declaration made on May 9, 1950, by Robert Schuman, France's Foreign Minister, whose family came from Lorraine—that region near the German border whose history is so redolent with Franco-German conflict. In this declaration, he proposed the pooling of French and German coal and steel resources under common institutions open to any other European countries able and willing to join.

Not everyone immediately grasped the significance of this proposal; but in restrospect it is clear that the Schuman Declaration contained, as well as foreshadowed, the essence of what was to come. Its aims were both long-term and immediate. In the long term, it sought to achieve European unity as a means to peace. "World peace," it declared, "can only be safeguarded by creative efforts which match the dangers that threaten it." "For peace to have a real chance, there must first be a Europe . . . Europe was not built, and we had war." It aimed, therefore, at "the European federation which is indispensable to the maintenance of peace."

To achieve this required, in M. Schuman's words, "the elimination of the age-old opposition between France and Germany"—between France and a Germany only then re-emerging as a nation from the nightmare of the past years and still divided into two halves, slave and free. It was vital to cement free Germany to the West. As M. Schuman said, "the solidarity . . . thus achieved will make it plain that any war between France and Germany becomes not only unthinkable but materially impossible."

To realize these long-term aims, it was necessary both

to solve particular problems, such as the future of the Ruhr and the Saar, and to make a breakthrough on a fairly narrow front. "Europe," declared M. Schuman, "will not be made all at once, or as a single whole: it will be built by concrete achievements which first create *de facto* solidarity." He went on: "The pooling of coal and steel production will immediately provide for the establishment of common bases for economic development as a first step in the federation of Europe, and will change the destinies of those regions which have long been devoted to the manufacture of munitions of war, of which they have been the most constant victims." "This transformation," he continued, "will make possible other joint actions which have been impossible until now." Among other things, "Europe will be able, with increased resources, to pursue the realization of one of her essential tasks, the development of the African continent." What was more, "Thus will be realized, simply and rapidly, the fusion of interests which is indispensable to the establishment of an economic community; thus will be introduced the germ of a broader and deeper community between countries long opposed to one another by bloody conflicts."

These quotations suffice to show that the Schuman Declaration was indeed a prophetic document. Today that "fusion of interests" is already taking place. We are ourselves achieving "the establishment of an economic community," part of whose resources are assisting "the development of the African continent." And there are already discussions about organized cooperation in other political fields than those covered by the European Economic Community, such as foreign policy, defense policy, and cultural affairs. In the political discussions we may perhaps see "the germ of a broader and deeper community"—or, as I think it might more appropriately be described, an organized political cooperation which may speed and assist the political integration implied in our European Economic Community. In all these respects, the Schuman proposals may be said to have gone according to plan.

In human affairs, of course, nothing goes *exactly* according to plan, and it would be naïve to suppose that the history of the last few years in Europe had seen the simple working-out of the project sketched in outline in May 1950.

Six countries followed the lead given by the Schuman Declaration. More would perhaps have done so had they been able to foresee its eventual outcome; but as it was, France, Germany, Italy, and the three Benelux countries negotiated and signed the treaty establishing a European Coal and Steel Community (ECSC), concluded in Paris on April 18, 1951. Its essential characteristics were that it was "supranational," that it was practical, and that it was partial.

The "supranational" aspect of the New Community was essentially what differentiated it from the "international" bodies already existing, the OEEC and the Council of Europe. To this question, and to this perhaps misleading term, I shall return in a moment. More to the point at present is that the Coal and Steel Community treaty was a very precise instrument with a very practical task, namely that of abolishing the economic effects of frontiers between its signatory countries in the sector of coal and steel, and establishing both transitional and permanent measures to enable all concerned to settle into the new situation of Community-wide competition. Finally, it is also important to remember that the Coal and Steel Community represented only partial integration: it concerned only coal, coke, steel, iron ore, and scrap, and excluded from its compass even related products like finished steel in such forms as steel tubes, to say nothing of all the variety of goods that take steel as their basis. It was thus an example of what was called at the time "sector integration," the breakthrough on a narrow front foreshadowed by the Schuman Declaration.

This points to a fourth characteristic of the Coal and Steel Community, one which it shares with all aspects and phases of the movement for European unity: that is, its evolutionary nature. Clearly, there were certain advantages, from the economic point of view, in pooling coal and steel. But the Schuman Declaration had made it clear that the process was not intended to stop there. Indeed, the Preamble to the Coal and Steel Community treaty, which echoed the Schuman Declaration, spoke of its signatories' "future common destiny."

What the next steps should be was for some time the

subject of intensive debate: it was thought, in fact, that integration in the field of coal and steel should be followed by the integration of other sectors of the six countries' economy. During those early days there were proposals for an agricultural community, the so-called "Green Pool"; for a transport authority; and for a health community, the so-called "White Pool." Little came of them at the time. Two further projects have a more important place in the story. These were the plans for a European Defense Community (EDC) and for a European Political Community (EPC).

The European Defense Community project, like the Coal and Steel Community, had both long-term and short-term aims. In the long term, it was seen by its sponsors as a rapid and dramatic means of making a further breakthrough in European integration, this time not in the economic field but in a jealously guarded domain that was highly and patently political. The plan provided for a European army of some forty divisions, wearing a common uniform, and in full liaison with NATO. This was to have been administered by common institutions similar to those of the Coal and Steel Community. Such a force, and such an explicit merger of national sovereignty, might have made an impressive contribution to the long-term cause of unity in Europe. And in the short term, this would have greatly strengthened NATO's existing fourteen divisions, in particular by calling upon Germany for her due contribution to the cause of common defense, in a way which would have countered the then common objections to the rearming of Germany or creation of a national German army— objections heard, it should be added, almost as frequently in the Federal Republic as elsewhere.

Article 38 of the EDC treaty, moreover, called for further steps toward political unity, to be studied in the first instance by the European Assembly which was to have been one of the EDC's institutions. In fact, however, even as early as September 1952, when the Assembly of the Coal and Steel Community first came into being, the six governments asked its members to co-opt further parliamentarians into a so-called "*Ad hoc* Assembly" in order to begin work on a draft political treaty without further delay. It was this *Ad hoc* Assembly which had the honor of first working out the project for a European Political Community which was to have crowned the institutions of both the Coal and Steel Community and the EDC.

Both these plans came to nought at the time. By the spring of 1954, it was true, four of the six national parliaments had voted to ratify the EDC treaty; but internal political difficulties, as well as a vehement propaganda campaign, partly directed by the Communist Party, had made it less and less likely that France would be able to do so. At the end of August 1954 the French National Assembly failed to ratify the EDC treaty. Thus fell the plan for a European Political Community. Although a brilliant last-minute rescue operation, partly inspired by Great Britain, helped to salvage some of the EDC's short-term military content—essentially by making possible a German defense contribution within the very loose framework of Western European Union—the political hopes that Europeans had placed in it seemed to be finally doomed.

Defeat, however, can sometimes be the school of victory. If, as it now seems, the failure of the EDC and EPC proposals marked the end of one stage in the uniting of Europe, and of one particular approach to unity, they also marked the beginning of another. Less than a year later, in June 1955, the representatives of the six member governments of the Coal and Steel Community met in Messina. On their agenda were three memoranda on the subject of further steps in European integration, one memorandum from Benelux, one from Germany, and one from Italy. Their final decision, like all such decisions, was a compromise embodying some of the views of all parties, but its essential element was that it set up a committee of national representatives to study possible methods of achieving further unity.

This intergovernmental committee produced its report the following April. One month later the Ministers of the Six adopted this report as the basis for negotiating two new treaties—for a European Atomic Energy Community (Euratom) and a European Economic Community (the Common Market). Within another ten months the treaties were signed; nine months later they had been ratified by all six countries; and on January 1, 1958, they came into effect. The speed of this achievement, which had as its starting point the lowest ebb of the European cause after the EDC debacle, was an eloquent testimony, not only to the ability of the men who were responsible for negotiating the new treaties, but also to the extraordinary power and resilience of the postwar European idea.

As I have said, this period marked a transition from one phase of the struggle for unity, and from one particular approach to its achievement. Let me explain. Essentially, the Coal and Steel Community treaty, and the EDC and EPC proposals, embodied the desire to move swiftly, almost spectacularly, toward the political goal of what M. Schuman had called "the European federation which is indispensable to the maintenance of peace." As such, they called for intensive action on a narrow front, and were concerned with the integration of particular sectors of national life, partly in response to particular and immediate situations—the problem of the Ruhr in the first case, and the problem of Germany's defense contribution in the other. This was the phase of what one observer has called "creative opportunism" in the postwar making of Europe.

With the two new treaties signed in Rome on March 25, 1957, there came the beginnings of a shift of emphasis. The Euratom treaty, it is true, was in some respects a further instance of "sector integration," but this time in a sector comparatively new and one which was therefore a *tabula rasa* by comparison with, say, coal and steel, in which national patterns of economic development had a very long history. But even atomic energy, apparently so limited in its scope, has ramifications in many other fields, ranging from questions of energy policy to matters of medicine and agriculture.

The Common Market treaty, for its part, covers not just one or two sectors of its signatory states' economy, but all sectors; and, as I shall attempt to show later, it covers matters of politics as well. In this respect, it is perhaps a more logical treaty than that of the Coal and Steel Community: it certainly embodies the concept of "economic community" first mentioned in the Schuman Declaration, and it carries it to its logical conclusion. Moreover, because its scope is so vast, it is perforce a different kind of treaty. Too, the Coal and Steel Community treaty did not provide the executive branch with powers to deal with external affairs. The Common Market treaty, on the other hand, foresaw the impact of an integrated European economy upon third countries and thus armed the executive organ with necessary authority in the field of external commercial policy. The Coal and Steel Community treaty, and in some degree the Euratom treaty too, are precise agreements laying down in some detail the objectives to be achieved and the methods to be adopted. For the whole of the economy of the member states, such foreknowledge and such precision would be impossible. The Common Market treaty is therefore very much more a treaty setting out general aims and establishing procedures and institutions to decide upon both the targets to be reached within this general framework and the exact means to be used. It is an exaggeration, but not much of an exaggeration, to say that from the purely technical point of view the Common Market treaty would have been capable of setting up, within its own framework, a European Coal and Steel Community or even an Atomic Energy Community. Indeed, by its recent decisions on agriculture, it has come close to establishing the so-called "Green Pool" that was first suggested in 1950. I say this not to belittle the achievements of either Euratom or the Coal and Steel Community, but to emphasize the difference I have mentioned.

Such emphasis is necessary, in particular, for a full understanding of the institutional structure of the three European Communities—or rather, of what is popularly and conveniently called simply "the European Community." In fact, the Coal and Steel Community, Euratom, and the Common Market share the same institutional framework; and because it is partly this which differentiates them from classical international organizations, the framework is worth examining in a certain amount of detail.

The Community's institutions have been called, with some legal justification, "supranational." This word correctly focuses attention on one of their most important characteristics, but it is also somewhat misleading in its overtones. It occurs, in fact, only once in the three Community treaties—in Article 9 of the Coal and Steel Community treaty, which calls upon the members of its executive body to "abstain from all conduct incompatible with the supranational character of their functions" and requires the member states to respect this obligation. The executive body is appropriately known as the "High Authority," again a term to be found in the Schuman Declaration; and its nine members, once appointed, are completely independent of member states, from whom they are forbidden to solicit or accept instructions. Their responsibility is to the Community as a whole. The same is true of the other two executive bodies, the Commissions of Euratom and of the European Economic Community, the former with five members, the latter with nine. All three executive bodies cooperate and share joint services in such fields as statistics, information, and law. It has been proposed, indeed, that they might be fused into one single body, perhaps with the title of "High Commission," a hybrid name compounded of their present separate denominations.

One of the problems to be faced in any such fusion, however, is the fact that the powers of the High Authority and those of the two Commissions are not quite identical. It is often suggested that the reason for this difference was a greater caution on the part of member governments at the time when the Euratom and the EEC treaties were negotiated. There may be some truth in this. The High Authority has a direct power of decision on most matters covered by the Coal and Steel Community treaty; only on questions of broader policy do decisions require the consent of the Council of Ministers whose members represent the member states. In addition, the

Coal and Steel High Authority is directly and independently financed by a levy on the coal and steel industries of the Community.

The EEC Commission, on the other hand, and in a lesser degree the Euratom Commission, have a power of decision which is more strictly defined, although it covers some quite important fields; and they at present draw their financial resources from pro rata contributions made by the member governments. The true role of the EEC Commission, in fact, is threefold. First, it has the task of drawing up proposals to be decided by the Council of Ministers; in this sense it may be said to resemble a United States Administration presenting bills to Congress. Second, it has the duty of watching over the execution of the treaty, and calling member governments and enterprises to account if they fail to respect it; in this function it perhaps resembles a federal regulatory agency. Third, the EEC executive has the role of helping to bring about agreement in the Council of Ministers, by using its overall viewpoint, its skill, and its power of advocacy, to secure the acceptance of measures which are in the interest of the whole Community, even if they mean temporary sacrifices of purely national interest. Here the EEC Commission might be said to resemble an Administration seeking to reconcile the various interests of the states.

Our Commission, then, is at once a motor, a watchdog, and a kind of honest broker; the word "executive," in fact, only vaguely describes it. But to conclude from this that the EEC must therefore be weaker than the ECSC seems to me to betray a basic misunderstanding of the European Community. As I said earlier, an important function of the EEC Commission is to help bring about agreement between the member states. In a sense, this is one of the main purposes of the whole institutional structure of the European Community. Unity, as history in Europe has shown us, is not something that can be imposed from above: solutions that ignore vital interests are not solutions. Nor, indeed, was it ever the intention of the Schuman Plan, or of the countries that accepted it, to establish in Europe a kind of remote technocracy ruling by ukase from some supranational kremlin. Despite its name, the High Authority has never been that. Rather, it was and is a body empowered to act impartially in execution of the more general decisions already reached by the member states during the negotiation of the ECSC treaty. Something of the same is true of the Euratom Commission. But as I have said, it was impossible for the member states to reach agreement, during the negotiation of the EEC treaty, on all the many fields involved in the integration of the whole of their economy. All they could do therefore was to establish a kind of constitution and leave the task of government to the various agencies for which it provided, hoping that the vitality of the Community's collective personality would make up for any lack of precision in the details of its mandate.

The second such agency, obviously enough, was the Council of Ministers. Given the circumstances I have described, it was natural and necessary that the Council, which comprises a minister from each member government, should share to a broader extent in the decision-making process of the EEC than in that of the ECSC. But here again some qualification is necessary. The Council of Ministers in the European Community seems in some ways to resemble that of a classical international organization, but in one important respect it represents an advance beyond this stage. The principle of majority voting is employed by the Community for its regular proceedings; the rule of unanimity, which was one of the stumbling blocks of previous experiments, is here reserved for exceptional cases which bear heavily upon national sovereignty in fields in which the principles of the treaty have to be made more precise in order to become directly applicable. Moreover, majority voting becomes more and more the norm for Council decisions as the treaty's transition period progresses. This again is only natural, not only because as time goes by the Community's sense of solidarity becomes that much greater, but also because in its early years one of the Community's principal tasks is to work out common policies, thus in a sense completing the negotiating procedure. From Stage Two of its transition period onwards—from 1962 onwards—such common policies are beginning to be applied. In the application of these policies, it may be added, the role of the executive becomes proportionately greater; and this again is a function of the general process I have described.

It may be in order here to say a word about the procedure of majority voting, since this is a question upon which the entry of new members directly impinges. In some cases, majority voting in the Council means a simple majority, with one vote for each member state. But in most instances, the rule of "qualified majority" applies. Under this system, France, Germany, and Italy, the three "big" countries, have four votes each; Belgium and the Netherlands have two each; and Luxembourg has one. To obtain a qualified majority, a total of twelve votes is needed in cases where the EEC treaty requires a proposal by the Commission; in other cases, the twelve votes must include favorable voting by at least four members. In practice, this means that where the Commission has made a proposal, no single member state can veto it, nor can the three Benelux countries. At least two countries and possibly even more are required to make up the necessary minimum of six contrary votes for a veto. On the other hand, unanimity is required to modify a proposal from the Commission; and in cases where the Commission is not required to make a proposal, the three "big" countries cannot overrule concerted opposition from the Benelux countries. This system therefore gives the smaller countries a certain guarantee, whose embodiment, so to speak, is the independent Commission. It also ensures that necessary decisions cannot be held up by

isolated opposition. Needless to say, the power of majority forms a very effective and essential incentive to reach
agreement. Although the arithmetic of qualified majori-
ties may have to be modified in the event of the entry of
new members, it is vital that the principle underlying it
be maintained.

The independent executives and the Council of Ministers, then, may be regarded as jointly forming the
decision-making agency of the European Community,
that is, its legislative agency responsible for issuing regulations. A third organ or institution of the Community
is the European Parliament, composed at present of 142
representatives and senators elected by and from the national parliaments, an arrangement comparable to the
former system for electing United States Senators. Each
of the Communities—the ECSC, Euratom, and the EEC
—has its own executive; and the Council of Ministers,
although in practice "shared" by all three, is legally
speaking three separate councils.

The European Parliament, however, is a joint body
formed by the legal amalgamation of the Assemblies provided for in the three Community treaties. Despite its
title, it is not strictly a legislative body, but it has the
task of exerting democratic supervision over the workings of the Community. This it does in three ways. First,
it has the right to be consulted on most major decisions
of policy. Its views have on several occasions led to mod-
ifications in the proposals put before the Council, and
therefore also in the measures finally agreed upon. Sec-

ond, its standing committees conduct periodic "hearings" at which the Community executives seek to explain their ideas and policies; and the Parliament, like the United States Congress, produces on this basis a number of extremely valuable and influential reports of which the Commission takes particular account. Third, the Community executives are required to report annually to the Parliament, which thereupon debates their activities. The Parliament may compel any of the three executive bodies to resign *en bloc* by means of a two-thirds majority vote of "no confidence." This substantial power has not yet been used against any of the Community executives; and some have criticized it as being too weighty a weapon to wield. Undoubtedly, the fact of its existence is important as an ultimate sanction, what one might call "a massive deterrent"; but there can be no doubt that as the Community develops it will be necessary to study ways and means of enlarging the Parliament's power.

The Community treaties already provide for the possibility of direct elections of members of the Parliament, and a project to this end has been prepared for consideration by the Council. Other suggestions have been made, but not yet codified into formal proposals. These include the possibility of giving the Parliament a greater measure of control over the executives' proposals, as well as a role in the appointment of their members. At the same time, on the Parliament's own initiative, the Council of Ministers has on several occasions appeared before it, although not specifically required by the treaties to do so;

and in some of our national parliaments, members of the European Parliament have not only consolidated their own reputations by their European activities, but have also acquired the habit of raising Community matters in questions to their own national ministers. In all these ways, despite the shortcomings inevitable in the evolutionary nature of the Community, the European Parliament is proving itself a real and positive force in the work of European integration.

There remains one final institution of the European Community whose function is more easily described. This is the Court of Justice, a Community Supreme Court whose word is law on all matters of interpretation of the treaties which make up the Community's Constitution. Like the European Parliament, it is common to the ECSC, Euratom, and the EEC. Its seven Judges are chosen for their acknowledged pre-eminence. Its function represents in some ways a blend of international and civil law, since it can settle both disputes between member states and actions involving any legal person within the Community. Its verdicts are directly enforceable by the domestic authorities of member states. It is perhaps superfluous to add that in the nine years since the Court began handing down decisions—most of them so far on coal and steel questions, but some already within the EEC—there has not been a single case of defiance of Court orders.

Such are the institutions of the European Community: Executives, Council, Parliament, and Court. As I have suggested, they bear the traces of their origin, and are not the net result of doctrinaire planning. Independent and impartial executives are clearly necessary where Community decisions must be taken quickly, and where the Community principle must be upheld. A Council of Ministers is equally vital as a means of bringing governments together, and ensuring responsible joint action in line with Community policy. If the executives are to be independent of national control by governments or parliaments, they must be subject to democratic supervision in the name of the Community's peoples; and if just and lasting traditions are to be established in this new framework, a Community Court is needed to ensure the rule of law.

The logic thus underlying the Community's institutional structure clearly bears some resemblance to that of a federation of states; and this analogy is in many ways a useful key to understanding the Community. Since the European Community is *sui generis*, a new kind of political animal, the analogy should not, of course, be pressed too far. Discussing the United States of America, Tocqueville anticipated the dilemma of those who today debate whether united Europe is federal or confederal, supranational or international: "The human understanding," he said, "more easily invents new things than new words, and we are thence constrained to employ a multitude of improper and inadequate expressions . . . A form of government has been found out which is neither exactly national nor federal . . . and the new word which will one day designate this novel invention does not yet exist."[4]

Just as language precedes grammar, so politics precedes political theory; and disputes as to the proper terminology for what we are doing in the European Community sometimes seem to me as academic as grammarians' controversies. On the one hand, nobody knows when European nations will find themselves in the same position vis-à-vis the Community as states of the American Union; yet on the other, they are clearly ready to contemplate a form of union going further than anything yet accepted in Europe. In this enterprise, to quote Tocqueville's words once more, "Another form of society is . . . discovered, in which several peoples are fused into one and the same nation with regard to certain common interests, although they remain distinct, or at least only confederate, with regard to all their other concerns."[5] How this "form of society" works in the field of economics I shall now attempt to describe, before finally turning to its political implications for Europe and for the world.

II
THE ECONOMICS OF EUROPEAN INTEGRATION

ONE OF THE ASPECTS of the United States that impressed Alexis de Tocqueville, as it has impressed visitors from Europe to this day, was the extraordinary degree of prosperity that he saw around him. "No people in the world," he declared, "has made such rapid progress in trade and manufactures . . . The Americans arrived but as yesterday on the territory which they inhabit, and they have already changed the whole order of Nature."[6] In the century that followed, the speed of this progress became even more striking. Between 1900 and 1938, United States industrial production rose by 163 percent; by 1955, the gross national product per head of population in the United States stood at $2,353, as compared with $1,109, less than half the American figure, in the European Community.[7]

Tocqueville attributed American prosperity in part to American energy and enterprise. "In the United States," he said, "the greatest undertakings . . . are executed without difficulty, because the whole population is engaged in productive industry, and because the poorest as well as the most opulent members of the commonwealth are ready to combine their efforts for these purposes." But there was also, he saw, another reason. He was economist enough to be familiar with the concepts of specialization and economy of scale; in another passage of his book he explicitly pointed out that "all commodities and ideas circulate throughout the Union as freely as in a country inhabited by one people. Nothing checks the spirit of enterprise."[8] In other words, the states of the American Union enjoyed in their commercial relations with each other the classical benefits of free trade.

The theory of free trade was already an old one when Tocqueville wrote. Indeed, in discussing American prosperity, he made what looked like concealed allusions to Adam Smith, Book IV of whose *Wealth of Nations,* published in the late 1770's, is in many ways the *locus classicus* on this subject. Since Adam Smith, the arguments in favor of free trade have been refined and qualified by a very considerable body of economic doctrine; but the core of the theory still stands. A distinguished British economist has summarized under two main headings the ways in which free trade may be held to raise the standard of living: "optimization of trade" on the one hand, and "maximization of production" on the other.[9] Others have put similar thoughts in another way. Pointing out that free trade in fact represents an enlarging of the market, they have stressed the economies of scale that this should make possible, in mass production and distribution, leading to lower costs. They have argued that large-scale producers would have easier access to sources of capital, bigger research and training budgets, better facilities for planning ahead, and in general greater stability. Competition on a wider scale should meanwhile stimulate modernization and eliminate inefficiency. At the same time greater specialization should lead to industries' being more economically located, and to each producing the commodities for which it is best fitted.[10]

Different advocates of free trade have emphasized different aspects of these general arguments, and some of them are now a little discredited. Nevertheless, history lends support to the thesis. The suppression of trade barriers in France, in the United Kingdom, in Switzerland, and in Germany was certainly accompanied by many of the benefits that free-traders predicted; and insofar as improvements in transportation may be regarded as a means of suppressing trade barriers, the same is true of the spread of the railroads and the growth of steamshipping.

On the world scale, however, free trade has so far remained a rather distant ideal. The nearest approach to this ideal was made in the twenty years following the Cobden Treaty of 1860; but by 1880 the goal had already begun to recede once more, and after 1914 it became still more remote. Part of the difficulty, no doubt, was that different nations, as the German economist

Friedrich List put it, "must modify their systems according to the measure of their own progress," adopting free-trade policies when these suited the state of their economy, and at other stages of their growth quite naturally seeking protection.[11] This is still generally recognized as the normal right of developing countries in the world today. In itself, however, it is only part of the general difficulties which beset any quest for world-wide free trade; and these difficulties have if anything increased over the last fifty years. In the words of Professor Jacob Viner, "The world has changed greatly, and is now a world of planned economies, of state trading, of substantially arbitrary and inflexible national price structures, and of managed instability in exchange rates. The classical theory is not directly relevant for such a world, and it may be that for such a world there is and can be no relevant *general* theory."[12]

In the Communist world, clearly, free trade is not to be expected; nor can Communist trade with the rest of the world be regarded as subject to free-trading conditions. Even outside the Communist world, moreover, governments now play a much greater role in determining the conditions of economic activity. To achieve the benefits of free trade, as I shall hope to show in a moment, something much more ambitious than the dismantling of classical trade barriers must be undertaken. Finally, the modern world acknowledges a number of social and political responsibilities, as well as new economic obligations, which free trade by itself can scarcely

be expected to meet. I am thinking in particular here of
the need to aid less favored sections of the Community
and developing nations of the world; but the same is true
of such delicate international economic problems as the
organization of agriculture and the search for stability in
markets where demand is elastic and production less
adaptable, as in the case of coal, or where, as in the case
of foodstuffs, supply fluctuates unpredictably against a
fairly constant pattern of demand.

In all these circumstances, despite the best efforts of
governments—and not least of the United States government—the postwar liberalization of world trade has
so far proved a very gradual and difficult process. The
Bretton Woods Conference of July 1944 marked the
beginning of a new effort to free and expand international trade; but the instruments that it created—the
World Bank and the International Monetary Fund—although achieving remarkable progress, fell short of their
founders' hopes. In 1946, again, the Economic and Social Committee of the United Nations set up the prepara-
tory body that drafted the Havana Charter; but its International Trade Organization was stillborn, and the
General Agreement on Tariffs and Trade (GATT), the
supposedly interim arrangement, did its best to fill the
gap. That "best" was quite remarkable, not only as a
testimony to the devotion and ingenuity of those who
served and still serve the GATT, but also as evidence of
a new liberal spirit on the part of its major participants,
and in particular, once again, the United States. It is not

to decry all this, however, to recall that in the early post-war years the results were still a long way from international free trade. It was partly for this reason that the same period saw various attempts to achieve free trade on a regional basis. Europeans, in particular, impressed as Tocqueville had been by the prosperity of the United States, began to wonder if they could not achieve a similar standard of living by establishing similar economic conditions, in particular a market of American size. This was one of the considerations underlying the formation of the Benelux union; it also motivated the abortive attempt to establish a customs union among the beneficiaries of Marshall Aid; and it is one of the complex of ideas embodied in the European Community.

You will have noticed, I am sure, that in turning to the question of regional free trade I have tacitly inserted the notion of the customs union. As Professor Viner has said in his masterly treatment of the subject, "The customs union problem is entangled in the whole free trade–protection issue, and it has never yet been properly disentangled."[13] Far be it from me to confuse the issue further or to tread upon ground already covered with such great insight and skill. But it will, I think, be generally admitted that given certain conditions—broadly that the customs union's "trade-creating" effects outweigh any "trade diversion"—the arguments in favor of a customs union are similar to those in favor of free trade. That is why, in referring earlier to commercial relations between the states of the American Union, I felt at liberty to speak

of "free trade" between them rather than their "customs
union."

Nevertheless, there remains a fundamental distinction,
which has to do more with the starting point of each
rather than with its ultimate goal; and this distinction is
neatly exemplified in the contrast between a customs
union and a free-trade area. A free-trade area, as defined
in the GATT, is one in which internal trade barriers are
reduced to zero, but each participant maintains its own
trade barriers and trade policy with regard to the rest of
the world. In a customs union, internal trade barriers are
reduced to zero as in a free-trade area, but all participants
adopt a common external tariff and a common policy for
external trade.

Ultimately, as I have suggested already, even to reap
the promised benefits of free trade it may be necessary
to envisage action in a number of other fields. But the
free-trade area formula by its very nature starts from
a different hypothesis. It sees the relationship between
its members as essentially that of independent partners,
each seeking to reserve to itself as much as possible of its
national prerogatives. The difficulty of doing so, however, is apparent in the familiar problem of "diversion
of trade." What would be the consequence, for example,
if the United States were a free-trade area rather than a
customs union? If Louisiana had a much lower tariff than
the state of New York? Clearly, if the difference in
tariffs were greater than that caused by transportation
costs, there would be a tendency for wide-awake busi-

nessmen to ship their goods into the United States through New Orleans, thus not only making the New York tariff meaningless, but also nullifying some of the economics of free trade by engaging in unnecessary transportation which would be artificially more economic than transit by the shortest route.

The classical solution to this difficulty is the imposition of internal levies which compensate for the differences in the external tariff by making such rerouting more expensive. This has the disadvantage that it tends to crystallize an existing situation and provide less stimulus to the transformations which give an economy its dynamism. Moreover, like all complicated systems, it may be subject to fraud. Above all, it emphasizes the differences between states rather than binding them in greater unity, and thus exemplifies the basic distinction between the theory of free trade and the theory of customs unions. For in a customs union the problem would not arise. The choice of New York or New Orleans as port of entry would be dictated—as indeed it is—by considerations of convenience and cost. As a result, there is one less barrier between the states concerned.

This simple example is in fact characteristic. A customs union, as its name implies, makes for union, and this in several ways. I have referred already to Professor Viner's seminal work on the subject. There is no need for me to reiterate the numerous examples that he has assembled to show the intimate connections between customs unions and political unions. It would be a rash man who would declare that the one is necessarily the condition or automatically the result of the other; it is never very clear whether "trade follows the flag" or vice versa. Nevertheless, most people would agree both that some continuing political will is necessary to the maintenance of customs unions, and that successful customs unions have in the past led to political unity.

To put the matter in these terms, however, seems to me somewhat artificial. It suggests that there is a fairly sharp distinction between "economics" and "politics," whereas the very phrase "economic policy," and even more so the older term "political economy," suggest on the contrary that the two are almost inseparable. "Geopolitics" is now a familiar concept; perhaps we need a similar word "economo-politics" to describe the frontier region I have in mind. For not only may customs unions *lead* to political unity; they may also *involve* such unity. Carry a customs union to its logical conclusion, in fact, and one finds that what it implies is economic integration. This in turn, as I shall hope to demonstrate, is itself a political phenomenon.

Writers on customs unions have long tacitly acknowledged the reality of this process. When, in 1915, Friedrich Naumann proposed a customs union between Germany and Austria, he pointed out that what he called the "economic state" thus created would try "to create a universally active exchange area. This involves an economic government directly responsible for certain economic legislation, while advising the national governments on the remainder. The direct functions of the economic government include customs, cartel regulations, export arrangements, patent laws, protection of trade-marks, control of raw materials, etc. Its indirect sphere of activity includes commercial legislation, social welfare and many other things."[14] In 1939, a British expert on the *Zollverein* likewise concluded that a customs union "can seldom be regarded as a permanent arrangement. Its members must sooner or later decide if they are to go backwards or forwards . . . If they go forwards they unify their economic organizations as far as possible. Common tariffs are followed by common systems of internal taxation—the same excises, the same direct taxes, the same monopolies. They adopt the same weights and measures, the same coinage, the same railway tariffs, the same code of commercial and maritime law, the same legislation with regard to the regulation of industry and workers."[15]

I myself would not carry the argument as far as this; nor would I agree on the order of priorities which it presupposes. A better formulation, to my mind, is that of a League of Nations study which was republished in 1947 by the United Nations. Its reasoning was summed up as follows:

For a customs union to exist, it is necessary to allow free movement of goods within the union. For a customs union to be a reality it is necessary to allow free movement of persons. For a customs union to be stable it is necessary to maintain free exchangeability of currency and stable ex-

change rates within the union. This implies, *inter alia*, free
movement of capital within the union. When there is free
movement of goods, persons, and capital in any area, diverse
economic policies concerned with maintaining economic
activity cannot be pursued. To assure uniformity of policy,
some political mechanism is required. The greater the inter-
ference of the state in economic life, the greater must be the
political integration within a customs union.[16]

These quotations demonstrate, I think, that the theory
of economic integration is not something new or something that has evolved ex post facto in the European
Economic Community. But the Community is a very
complete embodiment of this general philosophy, and
a full understanding of each is necessary for an understanding of the others.

As I pointed out earlier, the European Economic Community is itself a part of the postwar drive toward unity
in Europe. In this sense it may be regarded as a means of
establishing throughout the territory of its member states
as much as possible of the uniformity of economic conditions that normally obtains within a single country.
But this situation, as I have suggested, may also be the
logical conclusion of a full customs union; and one way
of considering the Community is to carry this logic
through to the end. Indeed, the technical basis of the
EEC is in fact a customs union; but unlike most such
agreements, it also provides—more or less explicitly according to the subject—for many of the other common
measures which are necessary to its full development as

an economic union, with all the political content that this implies.

Naturally enough, the customs-union provisions of the EEC treaty are among the most specific of its rules. It is comparatively easy, for example, to set a timetable for tariff reductions, which can be stated in percentages, but it would clearly be absurd to state, for instance, that "economic policies shall be coordinated by 50 percent on such-and-such a date." In fact, the treaty provides for customs tariffs between the member states to be gradually abolished over a twelve-year transition period, made up of three separate stages of four years each. During the same period, the member states' separate external tariffs are to be averaged out into a common external tariff surrounding the whole Community. This, according to the treaty, is to be achieved in three steps, one at the end of each four-year stage, so as to avoid the difficulties characteristic of a free-trade area. This parallelism, as it may be called, between the different measures required by the treaty runs right through its provisions.

Despite its name, a customs union cannot confine its attention to tariffs alone. It must also abolish, in trade between the member states, that other classical barrier formed by quantitative restrictions. These too, under the EEC treaty, are scheduled to disappear gradually during the transition period; and just as the Community's member states are to apply a common external tariff, so they must adopt by the end of the transition period a common policy in their external trade.

Tariffs and quantitative restrictions, however, are only the most obvious of the means whereby governments may nowadays restrict trade, distort competition, and in particular protect home markets and industries. Taxation systems, special legal requirements, subsidies and export rebates, credit guarantees, and even transport rates may also, deliberately or otherwise, have the same effect. To make a customs union real—to make it a true "common market"—these measures must be adjusted to ensure that they do not perform under another name the same task as tariffs and quantitative restrictions. Nor, indeed, does this apply only to government measures. Private firms may, for instance, artificially improve their competitive position by "dumping" in a neighboring country; they may also come to terms with their foreign competitors in market-sharing agreements or cartels which divide up the "common market" that the customs union aims to create. And monopolies, if they are large and powerful enough, may operate in much the same ways as cartels. To meet all these dangers, the EEC treaty provides for rules of competition which apply to governments and private firms alike, and which seek among other things to prevent the restriction or distortion of competition between the industries and products of the various member states.

But the treaty's provisions cannot apply only to goods. In order to obtain all the advantages promised by a customs union, it is equally necessary to liberalize the factors of production—capital and persons. Free movement of goods is meaningless unless they can be paid for; so current payments must be freed. There would be little hope of international specialization and division of labor if investments were not free to move to wherever they were most productive. The same applies, for economic as well as for human reasons, to the free movement of men and women. The EEC treaty therefore provides for the gradual liberalization of capital movement, the free movement of labor, and the removal of restrictions on the right of establishment in business and the professions and on the freedom to supply services throughout the Community.

Looking back, I find that I have used the words "free," "freed," or "freedom" six times in the last four sentences. Stylistically this may be regrettable, but it is also rather significant. What is offered, in fact, by those aspects of the European Economic Community that I have so far described is a great expansion of its citizens' freedom, for it involves the gradual demolition of national economic barriers which extend over some 1700 miles of man-made boundaries. This process of taking down the barriers, as I have said, is a gradual one. It has to be, in order to give all concerned the time to adjust to the new situation and to exposure to full competition from other Community countries. But at the same time, it is a process to which a definite time limit must be set in order to provide the incentive for adjustment, a time limit from which, for the same reason, there can be no turning back. That is why the EEC treaty, in providing for a transition period, limited it to twelve years, with an outside limit of fifteen. That is why, in contrast to most international treaties, there is no provision for opting out of the European Economic Community.

Even so, the EEC treaty recognizes that there may be particular transitional difficulties; and to meet them it provides not only for special temporary safeguard measures and escape clauses, but also for special measures of assistance. Broadly speaking, the latter are supplied by two Community agencies: the European Social Fund, for the retraining and resettlement of any displaced workers, and the European Investment Bank, whose tasks include aid for modernization or rationalization of production, as well as assistance to backward areas within the Community.

These provisions may be regarded as a human substitute for the famous "hidden hand" that Adam Smith hoped would smooth out economic difficulties. As such, they clearly go beyond the limits of classical economic theory. In other fields, too, the EEC treaty recognizes those limits and provides for positive policy-making in matters where the mere elimination of economic barriers is not enough. This is particularly the case in transportation and agriculture, where the establishment of a single market must be backed by additional safeguards and other measures because these are branches of the economy where competition and the free enterprise concept are greatly overshadowed by *dirigiste* measures of state planning and monopolies, subsidies, and other forms of artificial protection. Therefore structural change must be aided and planned as well as set in motion. Here, as in the field of external trade, the EEC treaty calls for common policies to supplement the more elementary and limited effects of greater competition.

Even this, however, is no real departure from the general philosophy of customs unions that I have already outlined: for that philosophy itself admits that dismantling economic barriers, with or without special aids and safeguards, is only a part of the task. In the words of the liberal economist whom I have already quoted, Professor James Meade:

We may conclude that the free movement of labor and capital within our economic union is in general to be desired in the interests of economic efficiency and of raising standards of living to the highest possible level. But in order that such an integration of the market for the factors of production, as well as for their products, should have this desirable effect, three conditions must be fulfilled. First, the individual member-states must not be too out of line with each other in their domestic policies concerning the distribution of income and property. Second, the individual member-states must not be too out of line with each other in their choice among direct controls, fiscal policy, and monetary policy for the stabilization of their domestic economies. Third, the individual member-states must not be too out of line with each other in those social and economic policies which determine their domestic demographic trends.[17]

In fact, the EEC treaty sets out among its objectives

the "progressive harmonization" of economic policies, and establishes a special committee to help coordinate monetary policy. Anticyclical policy, likewise, is to be considered "as a matter of common interest." The caution of the wording in these instances—as in those sections of the treaty which refer to collaboration on social policy—partly reflects, no doubt, the reluctance of national governments to tie their hands too tightly in advance. Partly, too, it springs from the general difficulty I mentioned earlier, that of setting precise targets and timetables for matters that are qualitative rather than quantitative. But it also indicates, in my view, awareness of the fact that if the full benefits of economic integration are to be achieved, work in these fields becomes inevitable. Since the EEC treaty, as I have said, is a treaty of procedures and principles rather than a set of precise and detailed instructions, it is capable of evolving the necessary particular measures as required—and they will be required. This is all the more so in that those who framed the treaty already knew, from the experience of the Coal and Steel Community, that adjustment to the new conditions of an integrated market is very much easier and more painless if wise and well-coordinated economic policies ensure the "steady and balanced expansion" for which the EEC treaty seeks to establish the basis.

Seen in this light, the lack of precision in these sections of the treaty—a lack which some have criticized— is in part at least a pledge of its signatories' confidence in its mechanism and in the gradual, ineluctable process of economic integration.

This confidence, of course, can only exist where there is similar confidence in the spirit of solidarity which the treaty represents. Put briefly, this solidarity is the willingness of the member states to pool not only their resources, but also their problems. In the political field, as I shall suggest later, it involves the willingness to renounce policies which would conflict with the vital interests of other member states—a kind of "loyalty to the union" whose implications in international law are even now the subject of study by jurists. In the economic field, this solidarity involves a readiness on the part of the member states to trust the Community method as a means to the solution of their own individual difficulties, and a corresponding readiness to treat their partners' economic problems as "matters of common concern," and hence partly as a responsibility of their own.

Such solidarity, obviously, is not to be created overnight. But one clear instance of it is embodied in the EEC treaty itself. This is the association of the so-called "overseas countries and territories"—the colonies and ex-colonies of Belgium, France, Italy, and the Netherlands, most of them on the African continent. By agreeing to their association with the Community, the member states acknowledged a joint responsibility for these countries' development. This joint responsibility is symbolized in a very concrete way by the fact that Germany, who was in the fortunate position of having no such dependencies, made as great a contribution to the overseas Development Fund as did France, with whom so many of the beneficiaries of the fund had intimate links.

I have said enough, I think, to show that the EEC treaty, although like all treaties a negotiated document, nevertheless represents a consistent economic philosophy. In some ways it resembles the classical philosophy of free trade; but it is not, as I hope I have made clear, merely a belated and anachronistic monument to Adam Smith. Nor, on the other hand, is it wholly or even in large part a *dirigiste* philosophy; it is much more flexible, and in important ways more liberal, than that. Broadly, it takes as its starting point the theory of the customs union. But just as this leads on quite naturally to that of economic union, so the EEC treaty provides for measures of economic integration, as well as for central institutions, which leave the classical notion of a customs union far behind. The political implications of this essentially evolutionary process I shall examine later. What I should like to do now is report on some of its achievements in the economic field. In accordance with the foregoing analysis, these may conveniently be considered under two main headings: (1) the dismantling of economic barriers, and (2) the forging of joint Community policies.

The EEC treaty came into force on January 1, 1958. Today tariffs between its member states have been reduced by 40 percent for industrial products, 35 percent for nonliberalized agricultural products, and 30 percent for liberalized agricultural products. This is ahead of the treaty's timetable; a further acceleration, with a further

10 percent tariff cut, may take place on July 1, 1962.*——
Similarly, the first moves toward the common external
tariff were made twelve months in advance of the required date, on December 31, 1960, but at a level one-
fifth lower than the treaty demanded—a provisional reduction anticipating the negotiations in GATT which
are now coming to an end. A second move toward the
common tariff may also be prepared in 1962 if a further
cut is made in tariffs between the member states. Finally,
in the field of quantitative restrictions, the Community
has moved ahead even more rapidly, abolishing practi-
cally all such barriers to the movement of industrial
goods by December 31, 1961, eight years in advance of
the original schedule.

In addition to this action on tariffs and quotas, the
Community has paid attention to other forms of restriction or distortion of its internal trade. Export duties have ⌐
been abolished. Taxes and fiscal duties whose effects are
similar to those of protective tariffs are being modified
or reduced. State monopolies are being shorn of their
protective or trade-distorting features; notable instances
of this are the changes in policies of the French and
Italian state tobacco monopolies, changes which have
greatly increased these countries' tobacco imports. Measures have been taken against dumping and certain state
aids. A thorough examination both of state subsidies
and of national turnover taxes is in progress, and further

* This was, in fact, done; on May 15, 1962, the EEC Council of
Ministers decided to make additional tariff cuts of 10 percent on
industrial goods (bringing the total internal tariff cut on such goods
to 50 percent) and of 5 percent on some agricultural goods, effective
July 1, 1962.

work on the broad questions of harmonizing legislation is in hand. On July 1, 1961, the Community imposed its ban on discrimination in transport rates and conditions based on the origin or destination of goods. And at the beginning of 1962 it issued its first detailed antitrust rules to prevent private firms from restricting or distorting competition within the Community.

Good progress has also been made in the liberalization of the factors of production. The first directive on the free movement of capital throughout the Community was issued on June 27, 1960, and a second is now under study. The measures so far taken fall short of full liberalization, because of the danger from speculative movements of "hot money" while the financial policies of member states are still divergent; but the Community's rules go further than the liberalization achieved by the OEEC—and further even than that outlined in its Capital Movements Code. Apropos the free movement of workers, a first regulation came into force on September 1, 1961; and a Community-wide system of guaranteeing the social security rights of those who move was established as long ago as 1958. Finally, on October 25, 1961, the Community's Council of Ministers approved twin programs for removing restrictions on the right of establishment and the freedom to supply services, programs under which many industrial and commercial activities will be liberalized by the end of 1963.

——The dismantling of economic barriers within the Community has already begun to make its effects felt. Trade

between the countries now members of the EEC was
already increasing rapidly before 1958, and from 1958
to 1961 it rose by 73 percent as against 27 percent for the
overall increase in the Community's trade with the rest
of the world. It would be rash, of course, to read too
much into these figures. But when seen in conjunction
with the countless modernization plans, specialization
agreements, and six-country associations in every branch
of industry and commerce, they seem to me to show that
the economy of the growing Community is responding
with remarkable *élan* to the new conditions created for
it. The Community's gross national product increased by
some 21 percent during the four years 1958–1961, and its
industrial production by some 32 percent. Present fore-
casts, moreover, suggest that, despite a slight slackening
of the phenomenal growth rate reached from mid-1959
to mid-1960, economic expansion is likely to continue
over the first half of 1962. Prospects for the second half
are less easily forecast, since they depend not only on the
economic and financial policies pursued by the member
states, but also on the business situation in the world and
particularly in the United States; but a further 4 to 5
percent increase in the Community's gross national product for 1962 is by no means beyond the bounds of possibility.

In these generally favorable circumstances, it has been
possible for the Community, as I have indicated, to accelerate the dismantling of its internal economic barriers,
and indeed to envisage the eventual possibility of actually

shortening its transition period. Whether this will prove feasible it is, of course, too early to say; but what is certain is that so far the Community countries have had little need to invoke the various safeguard and escape clauses written into the EEC treaty. Special measures have been taken, for example, in the case of Italian sulphur, raw silk, lead, zinc, and various chemicals; other cases include a temporary tax in Germany on Dutch bread and on Dutch and Belgian fondant paste, as well as a special *régime* for wine. Similarly, the use of minimum import prices for agricultural products has been comparatively limited. Nor, I may add, have the member states conspicuously failed in their obligations under the treaty. Insofar as infringement of its rules may be regarded as the use of "unofficial safeguards" such cases have been happily—and quite properly—few and far between.

Nevertheless, what I earlier called the human substitutes for Adam Smith's "hidden hand" have not been idle. The European Social Fund was brought into being in 1960, with resources of $30 million for the two years 1960 and 1961; it has received requests for aid totaling $25 million. The European Investment Bank, with a capital of $1 billion, has so far made loans totaling more than $120 million, making possible a total investment of some $900 million, the bulk of it in underdeveloped regions of the Community. I may also mention in this connection the European Development Fund for associated overseas countries, which out of a total of $581.25

million had by the end of 1961 allocated nearly $300 million for aid to African and other developing countries.

Some of the activities I have mentioned already enter into the second broad aspect of the Community's operations, that is, the forging of common policies. This is a field, as I have said, where progress is more difficult to chart—and also more difficult to achieve. Paradoxically, the conditions of economic expansion which the Community has enjoyed may even have added to the difficulty, by making the coordination of certain aspects of economic policy less evidently and urgently necessary. Joint action may sometimes be easier when danger threatens than in times of peace and plenty. Nevertheless, the Community's institutions are pulling their full weight in this domain too; and one index of the growing habit of joint consultation and coordination that they are fostering is the extraordinary number of daily contacts at all levels that are now taking place between officials and experts of our member governments, often under the aegis of the EEC Commission and in its Brussels offices. The Community's Monetary Committee has now been supplemented by a special Business Cycle Committee; Community Finance Ministers hold regular meetings; reports and recommendations on monetary policy, regional policy, social policy, fiscal policy, and even on bankruptcy laws continually help to bring minds and measures closer together. These are tasks that will become ever more necessary as the remaining economic barriers between the Community countries dwindle and disappear. But already, whether in formal conferences or in administrative committees, the groundwork is being prepared.

In those fields of policy where the EEC treaty is more specific, the Community's progress is correspondingly easier to define. In the matter of social policy, a time-table for equalizing rates of pay for men and women was agreed upon at the beginning of 1962; a little earlier the Commission drew up a series of proposals for voca-tional training; and elaborate studies are under way on almost all aspects of working conditions and wages within the Community. On transport policy, the Com-mission has made a first set of recommendations for modernization and development, most of which are now being implemented; it has drawn up a series of proposals for the broad lines of the common policy that the treaty calls for; and it has secured the agreement of the member states that they will consult together beforehand on any important measures of transport policy that they envisage from now on.

I have left until the last that field of common policy where the Community's progress has so far been the most striking—and not the least difficult to achieve. That, I need not remind you, is the thorny problem of agriculture.

In 1957, when we negotiated the EEC treaty, we all knew that to achieve a common market in agriculture was vital to the future Community. Agriculture accounts for about 12 percent of the Community's gross national product, and employs nearly a quarter of its working population. To leave it out of the process of economic integration would not only be grossly unfair, but would also be fatal to the balanced and comprehensive development of our economic union, and hence to any real prospect of building political unity. We also knew, however, that agriculture raised the most acute political and economic problems and that no previous efforts to perform the task we now set ourselves had come anywhere near success. In these circumstances it says much for the ingenuity and persistence of all responsible that early on the morning of January 14, 1962, after a final all-night session, the Community's Council of Ministers finally reached agreement on the first measures of a common agricultural policy. The courage of the ministers should not be underrated—nor, indeed, their endurance. Forty-five separate meetings, 7 of them at night; a total of 137 hours of discussion, with 214 hours in subcommittee; 582,000 pages of documents; 3 heart attacks— the record is staggering. It is also, I think, quite striking in its testimony to the whole spirit of our enterprise.

Of course, this is only a beginning. There are further problems ahead, in agriculture as elsewhere. I for one would not be surprised if we have further all-night sittings when we come to settle price policy for farm products, when we come to formulate a common energy policy, or when we reach the stage of concrete decisions in our common policy for external trade. But all worthwhile decisions are difficult. Indeed, it is by difficulties that we make progress, just as it is by means of friction that a vehicle moves forward.

Largely as a result of the decision on agriculture, our Community moved forward in January 1962 into Stage Two of its transition period. A contrary vote by any one member state would have sufficed to postpone Stage Two; but now the Community is past the so-called "point of no return." Further progress into Stage Three and on to the end of the transition period can only be slowed down, that is, if the Commission proposes a delay and if all the member states unanimously accept the proposal. Moreover, the principle of majority voting in the Council of Ministers, already in force for a number of important decisions, is now extended to a number of others, and in Stage Three it will be extended further still. If the customs union of the EEC was its most obvious feature during the first four years, it is the economic union which from now on will characterize the Community more and more.

Already it is clear that even the words "economic union" are inadequate to describe the European Economic Community. This is perhaps most apparent when one considers its relations with the rest of the world. Recent months have provided fresh confirmation, indeed, not only of its economic success, but also of its political significance and its growing power of attraction. Great Britain and other European countries, originally a little skeptical about whether the enterprise would work, have now decided to seek full membership in the Community; others, chary of this political commitment, are exploring the possibilities of association with it. Most recently of all, the United States, always an active supporter from afar, now seems to be moving toward a new "open partnership" with the European Community and other countries of the free world, a partnership which may transform the whole international scene. Treating of another subject, Alexis de Tocqueville wrote, "Whithersoever we turn our eyes we shall witness the same continual revolution throughout the whole of Christendom."[18] For my part, I believe that we are witnessing a "continual revolution" today, and one in which the European Community has no small share. Let us now turn to the political nature of that revolution.

III THE POLITICS OF EUROPEAN INTEGRATION

"A NEW SCIENCE of politics," said Alexis de Tocqueville, "is indispensable to a new world."[19] In my own view, as I have previously hinted, the very nature of this world necessitates a redefinition of what we ordinarily mean by words like "politics" and "economics," and a redrawing, perhaps even the elimination, of the semantic frontier between the two. "Economic integration" is a response to a political challenge, a political response that is also a political process. Moreover, the European Community that is being created forms a part of the "continual revolution" that is transforming our age. As such, it is not only a new economic entity, but also a new political fact which in its turn has political consequences in the wider world.

The essence of politics, however, is choice. I do not want, therefore, to give the impression that because the logic of economic integration is compelling and inexorable, its consequences can be put into practice without making a political choice and a number of difficult political decisions. Such choice and such decisions were needed before the process of European integration could begin. In order that it may continue, they are needed at every step of the way. And in order that an integrated Europe may make its full contribution toward solving the crucial problems that face us all, further political choice and political decisions will have to be made, not only by the European Community, but also by its friends, allies, and partners in the free world as a whole. That is why this book is subtitled "Challenge and Opportunity."

It was in response to a political challenge, of course, that Europe began to unite. I have already spoken of the technological challenge: the advent of mass production and hence of the need for larger markets; the relative shrinking of distances as communications improve; the emergence of new economic giants in the United States and the Soviet Union. Is it necessary to add that these new developments were political challenges too? The need for larger markets is itself a challenge to the narrower frontiers of the nation-state. The shrinking of distances reinforces the need for nation-states to acknowledge their mutual interdependence. The emergence of new giant powers is a constant incentive to the older—and smaller—nation-states to seek to preserve their influence by submerging their ancient rivalries in effective joint action.

All these political challenges are, or may be, peaceful. They would not be removed by banning thermonuclear tests, by securing world disarmament, by reaching a permanent pact with the Communist powers, or by channeling the forces of aggressive nationalism into pacific and constructive paths. In this sense, therefore, they are a permanent feature of our world's political landscape. Nation-states in the nineteenth century faced them, but failed to come to terms with them. Partly for this reason, our generation has been obliged to meet further political challenges which by their nature are sharper and very much more formidable.

The most obvious of these is the thermonuclear bomb; but this is only the supreme and symbolic example. National frontiers began to lose much of their military significance with the invention of tanks and aircraft half a century ago. Artificial satellites and intercontinental missiles have carried the process further. With destructive weapons so powerful and so indiscriminate as thermonuclear devices, war ceases to be an instrument of policy. From now on, the aim of diplomacy can no longer be to win the next war, but only to prevent it; and the aim of military policy can only be defensive and deterrent. In this new context, it was necessary in Schuman's phrase to make war between France and Germany "not only unthinkable but materially impossible." The "watch on the Rhine" has no meaning now, when all Western Europe is surely in the same boat.

This fact in turn is itself a reminder of a second political challenge, and one which takes the form of a political threat. There is no need to recall the various stages of disillusionment whereby that threat became apparent: the rapid establishment of Soviet hegemony in Eastern

Europe; the division of Austria and Germany; the abortive attempts at settlement; the civil war in Greece; the creation of the Cominform; the Zhdanov Manifesto; the Communist coup in Prague; the blockade of Berlin; the crushing of Hungary; the building of the Berlin wall. There is no need to recall the ceaseless war of nerves, the carefully timed concessions and blandishments, the suddenly renewed threats. Suffice it to say that for fifteen years Western Europe has been menaced by political forces whose explicit aim is the negation of democratic life. These forces are very close at hand: the Iron Curtain is nearer to Brussels than Washington, D.C., is to Boston. They are very powerful, and their strength is increasing. Moreover, they challenge us in all spheres. Restrained from overt attack by fear of the nuclear deterrent, Communist forces continually infiltrate in matters of economics and politics. "Competitive coexistence," in fact, means cut-throat competition; and it is competition in which Communist empire-building is backed by all the resources of central planning, and all the dynamism of a pseudoreligious sense of mission. To meet it, the West must prove that a free system based on reason and a respect for human beings can work even better—provided that artificial and anachronistic barriers to the free system are removed. Economic integration in Europe is a major step in this direction.

It is also a step toward meeting a third new political challenge, and one which future historians may come to see as the central issue of our epoch. This is the challenge and the opportunity represented by the emergence from centuries of domination and poverty of the proud new nations in Africa, in Asia, and in Latin America. Some of them look back to civilizations older than that of Western Europe; they all look forward, with justified impatience, to a material future comparable to that of the world's industrialized countries. That these new nations will avoid the tragic errors that our countries have made in the past is their hope, and ours. We owe it to them to demonstrate that we too have learned from past mistakes, and that a free and democratic society can provide solutions to their problems at least as rapid and effective as those promised by its antithesis.

All these, then, were political challenges to the West—and to Western Europe—to put its house in order. To meet them adequately required a political decision. As Schuman put it on May 9, 1950, "It is no longer the moment for vain words, but for a bold act—a constructive act." The rest of his declaration made it clear that its whole purport was political, and politically audacious. Five years after the end of World War II, it proposed political reconciliation—and progressive material integration—between France and Germany, working toward a "European federation." The immediate means appeared to be economic: "Thus will be realized, simply and rapidly, the fusion of interests which is indispensable to the establishment of an economic community." But the goal was clearly political: "Thus will be introduced the germ of a broader and deeper community between countries long opposed to one another by bloody conflicts."

Thus, right at the beginning of the story, its political nature was made clear. It would be hard to state it more unmistakably; and it was certainly understood by those European countries which for this very reason felt unable to respond to Schuman's appeal. Those that did were equally perceptive. They followed the Schuman Plan —the Coal and Steel Community—with two even more explicit and ambitious ventures, the Treaty for a European Defense Community and the draft project for a European Political Community. These ventures failed. More successful were the projects for a European Atomic Energy Community and for a European Economic Community. Present discussion of the possibilities for some form of organized cooperation among the member states of the European Community in other political fields than those covered by our Rome treaty is a further reminder that politics is the continuing theme of all these efforts. What precise shape such organized cooperation might take is as yet uncertain. However, no one envisages such cooperation as in any way a substitute for what is being achieved by the existing institutions of the European Community. Cooperation should assist, not hinder, integration.

Mention of the Community's institutions, indeed, is yet another reminder of the political nature of its work. Living and working within the structure of those institutions, one is sometimes tempted to take them for granted and to forget how unusual they seemed when they were first established. Three of them—the Executives, the Parliament, and the Court of Justice—are a clear acknowledgment of the unity of that larger entity which is being created; and the fourth, the Council of Ministers, although in some respects resembling a traditional international body, is also an integral part of the new and larger whole, not only in its legal status but also by virtue of its voting system and, I may add, the atmosphere and spirit that normally prevail there. Together, these organs have many of the characteristics of administrative agencies. They certainly amount to what the League of Nations experts on customs unions called "some political mechanism." Within their limits, indeed, they follow a federal pattern.

I said "within their limits." Lest this qualification be misunderstood, I would like to qualify it with a further quotation from Professor James Meade, whose study of economic union I have already had occasion to cite. He wrote: "It is altogether too simple-minded to argue . . . that we can form a federation or other type of economic union which transfers to some supranational body just one or two precisely defined economic functions and which leaves the national governments thereafter complete freedom in the design of their own domestic economic policies . . . The implications of economic union are much more far-reaching than that; and it is no accident that in the federal democratic states which really work in the modern world more and more economic power is passing from the member-states to the central union."[20]

These are the words of an economist. I myself would like to put it differently. The EEC treaty provides, in a number of very flexible ways, for joint action in the policy field. In certain places, particularly on social matters, it calls for "collaboration" between the member states. Elsewhere, especially on the question of general economic policy, monetary and financial policy, and the balance of payments, it speaks of "coordination," partly through the Community's Monetary Committee. Cyclical policy and exchange-rate policy it requires to be considered and treated as "matters of common interest." "Harmonization," on the other hand, is what the treaty requires in the field of tax policy; while in a number of other cases it calls for the "approximation" of national legislation. Apropos competition—including antitrust questions—the treaty demands "common rules"; and for agriculture, transportation, and foreign trade it specifically stipulates that "common policies" should be applied.

All these are pragmatic provisions, but they are, I think, highly significant. In my view, the logic of economic integration not only leads on toward political unity by way of the fusion of interests; it also involves political action in itself. What, in fact, are all the matters that I have just mentioned if they are not political? What issues could be more burningly political than those of agriculture? The member states of the European Economic Community have agreed to face them together, and they have already reached unanimity on the beginnings of their common agricultural policy. What economic question is more deeply involved with the political issue of national sovereignty than that of exchange-rate policy? The Community's member states are pledged to treat it as a matter of common concern. Finally, what could encroach more openly upon national autonomy than the establishment of a common policy for external trade? At the end of the EEC's transition period, this will be subject to majority vote.

Once again, let me stress that I am not suggesting that all this will follow automatically or without snags. In politics nothing does. Agreement on all these matters will require political courage certainly no less than that which was needed to sign the Community treaties in the first place. And that courage was considerable, for the treaties set in motion a process far more ambitious than the modest words "economic integration" would suggest. What they provide for, indeed, is the integration not of economic activity as such—the actions of employers, workers, producers, merchants, professional men, and consumers—but of the increasing role played by government in determining the conditions within which such economic activity takes place. We are not integrating economics, we are integrating policies. We are not just sharing our furniture, we are jointly building a new and bigger house.

"Political integration" is not too bold and too grandiose a term to describe this process; in the long run, as I have suggested, its starting point, its goal, its methods, and its subject matter all lie within the political domain. The significance of this becomes clearer when one turns to consider not the domestic policies of the European Community's member states, but the relations of the Community as a whole with its partners in the rest of the world.

A transformation of those relations was of course one of the major aims of building the European Community —a new giant big enough to hold its own in a world of giant powers. Perhaps for this reason, the EEC treaty is almost surprisingly unspecific in this domain. It contains a number of declarations of principle, stating, for example, that the Community is "desirous of contributing . . . to the progressive abolition of restrictions on international trade" and that it wishes "to ensure the development" of the prosperity of overseas countries "in accordance with the principles of the Charter of the United Nations." To these ends, it calls in particular for a common policy in matters of external trade, and for the association with the Community of overseas countries and territories having "special relations" with the member states. It affirms the member states' willingness to enter into "reciprocal and mutually advantageous arrangements directed to the reduction of customs duties below the general level which they could claim as a result of the establishment of a customs union between them-

selves"—a clear pledge that the Community's common
external tariff is a starting point for further tariff reductions. As regards quantitative restrictions, the treaty de-
clares that "Member States shall aim at securing uniformity between themselves at as high a level as possible
of their lists of liberalization in regard to third countries
or groups of third countries"—a call for external policies
to move in the direction of the most liberal policies then
practiced, rather than the reverse. To achieve these general aims, the treaty provides for some general rules and
procedures; it also provides for the possible accession of
new member states, as well as for the negotiation of possible association agreements with other countries or
groups of countries, embodying the exchange of rights
and obligations between them and the Community as
a whole.

All these, I think, may be regarded as liberal provisions and declarations of intent. That this is so, and that
there is no separate part or title of the treaty exclusively
devoted to foreign economic policy as such, is a reflec-
tion of the treaty-makers' confidence that the very fact
of creating the Community would in itself be a major
contribution, not only to the world's political and economic stability, but also to the increase of its prosperity
and the expansion of its trade. The formation of a customs and economic union in Europe, it was thought,
would lead to rapid economic expansion within the Community, which in turn would increase its imports from
the rest of the world; the abolition of protective bar-

riers between the member states, obliging their industries to become competitive with each other, would enable them to pursue more liberal policies vis-à-vis non-member countries; and the existence of the growing Common Market would act as an incentive for the negotiation with it of mutual tariff reductions which would benefit, and help unite, the whole of the free world. The resultant reordering of international economic relations, it was thought, would enable the Community and its partners to bring new forces to bear upon the world's outstanding problems—such as those of trade with the Communist bloc, of world agriculture, and of effective and comprehensive aid for countries in course of development. In this wider context, the European Community could be seen not only as a European response to political and economic challenges, but, what is much more important, also as a new dynamic in its own right, an important factor in a further political and economic process whose possibilities were boundless. If it was a challenge to established habits of thought and action, it was also a great opportunity.

Something of this the Community itself declared at the time of its creation. It pointed out, first, that it was in full conformity with the rules of the existing international organizations to which its member states belonged, in particular, the OEEC and the GATT. Both the OEEC and the GATT permitted and indeed encouraged the formation of customs unions; the only proviso was that the external tariffs of such unions must be no more protective than the previous tariffs of their individual member states. The Community's tariff, based on the purely arithmetical average of its members' national tariffs, in practice meant a very substantial lowering of the protection surrounding the French and Italian markets, with some 90 million consumers; the maintenance of roughly the same protection around the German market of some 50 million; and a tariff increase only for the Benelux countries, with a population of little over 20 million. Even arithmetically, the incidence of the common tariff was lower than that of the national tariffs it replaced. Some duties—those of the famous "List G" in the EEC treaty—remained to be fixed by negotiation among the member states; the outcome here too was a lowering of previous protective barriers.

The association with the Community of overseas countries and territories was a further subject of debate. Under the EEC treaty, the Community countries were gradually to lower to zero all protective barriers between them and the associates, while the associates were to extend to all member states the preferences they granted to their former mother countries. This amounted to the establishment of a free-trade area between the Community on the one hand and the associates on the other. The normal disadvantages of such arrangements were for the most part avoided in this case because of the nature of the products concerned and because permission was granted to the associates to levy revenue duties and even protective duties for the safeguard of their infant industries. A free-trade area, like a customs union, is of course legally permissible under the rules of GATT, which in both these cases waive the normal requirements of their most-favored-nation principle. In this respect also, therefore, the EEC felt itself fully justified from the legal point of view. I am glad to say that this feeling has since been confirmed, not only by the acquiescence of the GATT, but also by the findings of an American scholar who has thoroughly investigated the whole thorny question.[21]

It ill behooves a lawyer like myself to admit that law is not everything, but it would be less than honest to pretend that for many anxious observers outside the Community, proof of the Community's legal conformity with the GATT was enough to show that it was beneficent. Nor, indeed, were its liberal professions of faith. It is only natural, after all, to be somewhat suspicious of mere words; and the animated discussions in GATT toward the end of 1957, even before the EEC treaty was in force, were only the beginning of a long debate, to which for some time the Community could make only hypothetical contributions, partly because the fears it was expected to meet were themselves hypothetical. The Community's critics, for example, complained that it would harm their exports; in the absence of any proof either way the Community's spokesmen could only reply that this was neither their intention nor their expectation, and that should any real damage occur as a result of the "discrimination" inherent in any customs union or free-trade area, they would be glad to seek remedies for it in consultation with their trading partners.

At the same time, moreover, a similar debate took place within the OEEC. Fearing the consequences of this so-called "discrimination," Great Britain and the other members of the OEEC proposed the formation of an OEEC-wide free-trade area for industrial products, negotiations for which continued almost until the end of 1958. The history of those negotiations is too familiar to require retelling, but the reasons for their failure are relevant enough to my present subject to be worth recalling at this point. I mentioned earlier some of the technical difficulties involved in establishing free-trade areas, and some of the conditions which in my view are necessary to secure the benefits of free trade. These difficulties were increased, in the case of the OEEC project, by the fact that it sought to set up a very loose and merely partial free-trade area of which the Community would have been one member, but at exactly the same pace as the latter's own process of internal tariff-cutting, and by means of negotiations in which only the individual Community countries, not the Community as such, were fully represented.

Reinforcing these technical difficulties, of course, were direct contrasts of material interest such as occur in any negotiation: the fact, for example, that some Community industries feared the immediate impact of new competition from outside the Community at the same time as that from other member states; and the fact that Great Britain, standing at the crossroads of an industrial free-trade area in Europe and a partly agricultural system of Commonwealth preferences, appeared to be getting the best of both worlds without giving comparable advantages to producers—and especially to farm producers—in the Community. But conflicts of interest of this kind, and even perhaps the technical difficulties, might not have sufficed by themselves to make impossible negotiation of the OEEC free-trade area had the project not faced in addition two political obstacles, both of them deeply enmeshed in the technical and theoretical problems I have described. The first was the danger that within such a wider, looser, and much more partial scheme the Community itself might have dissolved, ceasing to be what was a then potential political entity, and becoming a mere commercial arrangement indistinguishable from the free-trade area, and thus incapable of giving it the continued political impetus necessary to achieve the benefits of free trade. The second was the fact that the proposed free-trade area would in turn have constituted an even greater area of "discrimination" without the political guarantees and advantages of the European Community. A major victim of this increased "discrimination," moreover, would have been the United States, which had tolerated quota discrimination against the dollar area by the members of the OEEC when their economies were still suffering from postwar weakness, but which would now have been asked to countenance tariff discrimination by them at a time when their currencies had again become almost fully convertible, and when the United States itself was beginning to suffer from balance of payments difficulties.

It was this consideration among others that led many people in the Community to favor what was then called "the world-wide approach." Essentially, this meant accepting the Community for what it was, and for what it would become. "Discrimination" was one thing if it meant merely capricious differentiation, applying different treatment to the trade of different countries for no other object than immediate commercial gain: it was quite another thing if it meant the gradual elimination of barriers between countries intent upon building a union an inevitable and necessary feature of which was "discrimination" of this kind. Obviously, and especially during its early days, the members of such a union would be under strong pressure to hold back from the pursuit of their appointed course, and to make a whole series of bilateral, regional, or even preferential "deals" with other countries in order to quiet the fears that the Community's emergence aroused. But, one could not help asking, might it not prove wiser and in the long run more beneficial all around for the Community to place a greater emphasis on its own consolidation, securing its own acceptance and that of its common external tariff, rather than perforating it with too many exceptions? Might not the Community then become a more effective lever both to help achieve a greater degree of liberalization in world trade and to help solve some of those other economic problems of which trade liberalization was only one factor and to which freer trade was a scarcely adequate solution?

This was the question that faced the European Community during the negotiations for an OEEC-wide free-trade area; and it clearly demanded a political choice of some magnitude and no less courage. That choice, of course, need not be exclusive. A world-wide approach need not preclude a certain number of special arrangements to meet particular cases. These could take the form of the kind of consultation already proposed in the case of any real damage to exports to the Community, either from GATT members in general or from the members of the OEEC. They could, on the other hand, go as far as the conclusion of association agreements, for instance involving a customs union such as that negotiated with Greece—a NATO member, a developing country, and one exposed to strong economic and political pressure from the countries of Eastern Europe. For this reason, I prefer to speak of a "pragmatic" approach to these problems, of which the main guiding lines are those I have described.

This approach, like the Community's liberal declarations of intent, was treated somewhat skeptically at the time. Only gradually, in fact, did the realities of it begin to make themselves felt. The first hint, perhaps, came when the Community proposed to extend to its trading partners—first in the OEEC, and then, significantly, in the GATT—a part of the first mutual reduction of trade barriers between its member states. A second and more telling indication was the Community's immediate acceptance of the proposal made by Mr. C. Douglas Dillon for negotiations with a view to reducing the tariffs of GATT members by some 20 percent. A third proof that the Community was in earnest was its anticipation of these negotiations by effecting the first accelerated moves toward its own external tariff at a level already provisionally reduced by the 20 percent proposed by Mr. Dillon. Happily, the so-called "Dillon negotiations" are now successfully concluded with most of the participating countries, including the United States, and the bulk of this tariff reduction has thus been confirmed. Moreover, the Dillon negotiations themselves were preceded, as they had to be, by negotiations under Article 24, Paragraph 6 of the GATT, whereby the GATT's contracting parties accepted the Community's common external tariff—a further vindication of this general approach and a further confirmation that the Community was now recognized as a new economic entity and a new political fact.

After four years' experience, indeed, it is beginning to be possible to draw some tentative conclusions on the subjects which so troubled the early months of the Community's life. The economic expansion which I described earlier has helped to vindicate those who claimed that, far from causing economic disruption, the process of integration would itself provide a new dynamic. The immense increase in internal trade between the Community's member states has helped to show that its "common market" is a reality. That this is in turn a trade-creating process which also benefits the Community's partners in the rest of the world is shown by the fact that the Community's external trade over the four-year period from 1958 to 1961 expanded more rapidly than that of any large country in the West.

From 1958 to 1961 the total imports of the United Kingdom increased by 17.5 percent; its total exports, by 16 percent. The comparable figures for the United States were 19 percent and 15 percent. Over the same period the European Community's total imports from the rest of the world rose by a full 27 percent, from just over 16 billion dollars' worth to well over 20 billion, and its exports increased at about the same rate. Much of this extra trade, moreover, was done with the United States, whose imports from the Community increased by some 34 percent. These increased imports by the United States were more than paid for by her vastly increased exports to the Community, which rose by no less than 44 percent. In 1958 the United States had a trade surplus with the Community countries of more than 1.1 billion dollars; by 1961 this had increased to more than 1.8 billion. This, I need hardly add, has done much to alleviate the United States's balance of payments position; and, as the rising standard of living within the Commu-

nity increases not only demand in general but more specifically the demand for high-quality American products,
this encouraging trend promises to continue.

In these ways, then, recent practical experience seems
to confirm the confidence the Community's spokesmen
have always expressed in its beneficent effects—the almost automatic corollary of the economic arguments in
its favor which I outlined earlier. I am not suggesting,
of course, that this process is wholly automatic, or that
there may not be individual exceptions to it, or indeed
that it would necessarily continue in the face of a world-
wide economic recession. What I think is clear, however, is that many of the fears expressed at the outset
both inside and outside the Community were very much
exaggerated; and that economic expansion within the
Community very much helps to offset and even remove
whatever problems "discrimination" poses for nonmem-
ber countries. But this is not all. It is my belief that the
very establishment of this large new economic entity can
ipso facto help to bring about a new stability in markets
and prices, as well as what the EEC treaty calls "a con-
tinuous and balanced expansion," which in themselves
greatly reduce the risk of a general recession. This is
partly due to the mere existence of the Community and
of the psychological climate that it helps to create. It
can be greatly furthered by the pursuit of wise and
forward-looking policies, not only by the Community itself, but also by its partners in the rest of the world.

A common policy for external trade is, as I have said,

one of the requirements of the EEC treaty. The need for this is so obvious, indeed, that, to adapt the epigram, if that chapter of the treaty did not exist it would be necessary to invent it. The establishment of a customs union as such, in fact, implies the application of a common commercial policy, for a union whose external policies were united only in the tariff field would encounter in all other fields many of the problems which beset a free-trade area. If each of the member states applied a separate policy in its external trade, even the internal aspects of the union might be imperfect, because at the internal frontiers it might be impossible to maintain the principle of free circulation for imported goods. Such technical considerations apply with even greater force to an economic union like that of the EEC. Moreover, just because one reason for creating the European Community is to enable Europe to play its full part in world affairs, it is vital for the Community to be able to speak with one voice and to act as one in its economic relations with the rest of the world. Only thus can it make its full contribution toward solving the problems that face it and its partners.

Under the treaty, a common policy in this field need not be fully applied until the end of the transition period; but in practice, negotiations in the GATT and elsewhere have already obliged the Community to develop certain practical features of its external trade policy, if only to make good its liberal declarations of intent. The Community began in 1961 to take the first formal steps in this

direction, by establishing a procedure for prior consultation between the member states whenever one of them
begins negotiations for bilateral trade agreements or plans
to change its liberalization system, and by stipulating
both that any further bilateral agreements shall not last
longer than the EEC transition period and that they shall
contain a "Community clause" providing for their trans-
fer to a Community basis. These first steps, agreed to by
the Council of Ministers in July 1961, may soon be followed by others if the Council accepts a further series of
proposals recently made by the Commission. These in
particular envisage the progressive alignment and increase of liberalization; the alignment of quota policies
vis-à-vis nonmembers of the GATT; the alignment of
antidumping measures; and the alignment of export arrangements including export aids. The aim of all these
measures is that set out in the treaty—namely, the har-
monious development of world trade and the removal
of restrictions upon it.

The beginnings of the mechanism for a Community
foreign trade policy are thus being set in place. What
its tasks will be I shall return to in a moment; before
doing so I should like to set the scene for it by recalling
two major political developments which help determine
the conditions of its application. Both are interlinked, and
both form a part of that "continual revolution" which
I mentioned earlier and which the creation of the Community has helped to trigger. The first is Great Britain's
application for full membership in all three European

Communities: the EEC, the ECSC, and Euratom. The second is the proposed Trade Expansion Act submitted to Congress by President Kennedy early in 1962.

Great Britain's application for membership in the European Community was in some respects the most striking testimonial to success—and to its political character—that could have been imagined. It was also, in my opinion, a vindication of the "pragmatic" approach which the Community adopted after the failure of the negotiations for an OEEC-wide free-trade area, an approach which had never excluded, and indeed had always recalled, the principle of the "open door." For the British government, it was an act of political courage, because it represented not only the recognition of those hard political and economic realities which had already encouraged the Community's existing members to strive for greater strength in unity, but also the deliberate reversal of Britain's age-old policy of seeking to maintain, and to help determine, a balance of power in continental Europe.

The Community for its part welcomed the British request for membership; and I should like to add that all the contacts that we have had with the leaders and members of the British negotiating team have confirmed this feeling, and confirmed too our regard and our respect for them. The atmosphere, as official communiqués put it, is excellent. I say this because the length and difficulty of the present negotiations may sometimes, perhaps, give rise to false impressions. If the negotiations are lengthy, it is because the ground to be covered is immense; if they are difficult, it is because the problems themselves are difficult.

One of the main complications arises from the fact that the Community itself, though successful, is still comparatively young. This gives any new adherent a greater opportunity to influence the common policies in their formative years, but it also means that the Community's existing members have to accelerate the coordination of their own individual policies in order to arrive at a common basis on which to negotiate. This, in a sense, means that they have to start tackling all their problems at once, and under considerable pressure.

This would be true of any application for membership coming at this stage, but it is particularly true in the case of Great Britain, partly on account of her Commonwealth ties, and partly on account of her more recent commitments to her fellow members in the European Free Trade Association (EFTA). The Commonwealth's importance as a political factor is certainly recognized by the Community. Its existing commercial arrangements with Great Britain, however, involve the present negotiations in a whole series of world problems, including aid to developing countries, outlets for tropical products, the treatment of low-wage manufactures, the stabilization of raw-material markets, the organization of temperate agriculture, and the avoidance or the disposal of farm surpluses. In the further connection of the Sterling Area, it also involves economic policy and world monetary problems; and even this list is incomplete.

The European problem raises further issues both economic and political. Denmark is now negotiating for membership in the Community, and Austria, Sweden, and Switzerland have applied for what would seem to be association with it. Portugal and Norway are so far undecided.* In addition, Ireland has applied for full membership, and Spain has applied for association with a view to eventual membership. I need not remind you that some of these countries, for various reasons, are neutral, and that several of them, economically, are still in the course of development. Nor need I add that they present the Community with a series of very difficult decisions, involving among other things some of the considerations that I mentioned earlier in connection with the formerly proposed free-trade area.

It would be out of place to try to predict here what those decisions will ultimately be—or, indeed, to report in any detail upon the current progress of the negotiations. Nevertheless, I think it may be said that to all the problems involved there are both bad solutions and good solutions. Within the Community, bad solutions would be those that weakened, disrupted, or divided the enlarged common market, that made national exceptions to its common policies, or that prejudiced its chances of further development toward unity. In external policy, bad solutions would be those that crystallized or increased commercial preference systems, that discriminated among

* Norway has since applied, on May 2, 1962, to negotiate for membership in the Community; and on June 4 Portugal requested negotiations with a view to establishing terms of collaboration with the Community.

the Community's friends and allies, or that halted the "continual revolution" that is leading to greater unity in the free world. Good solutions, on the other hand, would strengthen and further unite the Community, and at the same time enable it and its partners to apply effective world-wide solutions to some of the major economic and political problems of our day, many of which are deeply involved in the present negotiations themselves. Will we succeed? It is against the rules in any negotiation to say so, but for my part I am confident that satisfactory solutions are possible.

The prospect of British membership in the European Community, then, is a further stage in the "continual revolution" of which the Community's creation was an early factor. A still further stage, and one that was surely prompted by that prospect, was opened early in 1962 by President Kennedy's request for additional negotiating authority under the Trade Expansion Bill. Hitherto, the President's authority has of course been limited by the Reciprocal Trade Agreements Program of 1934 and more specifically by the Trade Agreements Extension Act of 1951. These limitations, as the Dillon negotiations showed, could be a serious hindrance to liberal policies. In the Dillon negotiations, "peril point" provisions at one time threatened to remove 220 million dollars' worth of trade from the bargaining process and might even have caused the talks to break down. The Trade Expansion Bill would give the President power to negotiate for tariff cuts of up to 100 percent on items where the

United States and the European Community together account for at least 80 percent of world trade, as well as on tropical agricultural and forestry products, and of up to 50 percent on other commodities.

It is certainly not for me to comment in detail upon proposals which at present are the subject of debate by Congress. I should like to say, however, that there is no doubt in my mind that these proposals potentially mark a revolutionary step forward. They seem to me to prove, first, that the United States Administration is more than ever determined never again to revive the policies of protectionism and isolationism which are now no longer appropriate—if indeed they ever were—to the world in which we live. Second, President Kennedy's proposals, like the actions of both President Truman and President Eisenhower, clearly recognize the existence and the importance of the European Community as both an opportunity for American exporters and a challenge to their dynamism and skill. Finally, it seems to me, the Trade Expansion Program is itself both a challenge and an opportunity for us all, and one which if handled properly could lead to a new and creative approach to many of the economic and political problems that face the free world.

Let me expand a little upon this last point. We in the European Community noted with great satisfaction, as I am sure did our friends in other countries, the particular stress that President Kennedy laid upon the nondiscriminatory character of the Trade Expansion Bill. Clearly, it is incumbent upon us all to ensure that in liberalizing world trade we do not pursue merely sectional or national interests, or those of the industrialized countries alone. We must respect both the letter and the spirit of the most-favored-nation principle enshrined in the GATT; and we must perform our mutual tariff-cutting in such a way that it neither in principle nor in practice discriminates against our other friends in the free world. That is why we for our part were particularly encouraged when President Kennedy described his proposals as the way toward an "open partnership," with emphasis on the word "open."

But tariff cutting as such is only a part of the "continual revolution" to which I have referred. President Kennedy's trade proposals include the possibility of "trade adjustment" measures which are designed to help industry adapt to the new situation, and which thus implicitly acknowledge that economic change, not merely commercial bargaining, is here in question. In this context I should like to quote the report prepared for Congress in January 1962 by the Subcommittee on Foreign Economic Policy, entitled "Foreign Economic Policy for the 1960's." It declared: "A commitment to freer trade is not just a commitment to lower tariffs. It is also an implied commitment to a rate of growth which approximates that of our partners; an implied commitment to a farm policy which encourages competitive trade and discourages burdensome surpluses; an implied commitment to a monetary policy which encourages growth while preserving the purchasing power of the dollar; and an implied commitment to a fiscal policy which stimulates high levels of employment and economic productivity."[22] To carry the report's argument into foreign economic policy, I am not at all sure that even a partial reduction of tariffs, if it is to be effective, may not necessitate something of the coordination of policies that I earlier suggested was necessary in the case of full free trade. Hence, the need for "open partnership" is a recognition of growing economic interdependence; and this time the emphasis falls on the word "partnership."

Many people have chosen to call this partnership the formation of an "Atlantic Community"; I prefer the formulation proposed by President Kennedy. In fact, when I hear the words "Atlantic Community," I am sometimes reminded of Voltaire's remark about the Holy Roman Empire—that it was neither holy, nor Roman, nor an empire. The so-called "Atlantic Community" cannot be confined to the Atlantic area, for its effects must embrace our other friends and partners in the Pacific and elsewhere. Nor is it a community in the same sense that this word applies to the European Community—that is, a full economic union, one new Atlantic personality, with integrated institutions and strong political implications. Whatever the degree of our interdependence, it would be unrealistic to expect our American and other friends outside Europe to assume all the obligations of the European treaties, with all their political overtones. What seems much more likely to emerge, in fact, is a close partnership between two personalities, the European

Community and the United States, benefiting not only its "partners," but the other countries as well.

Already, we have at our disposal the instruments of such a partnership, in the GATT and the Organization for Economic Cooperation and Development (OECD). The GATT is working well, both as a code of good conduct and as a broad negotiating forum. Its efforts, already stimulated by the creation of the European Community, will certainly be facilitated if the Trade Expansion Bill becomes law. But modern economic conditions, as I have already suggested, require more positive policies and institutions to apply them. Such a role may well be played by the Organization for Economic Cooperation and Development, which the United States and Canada helped the European countries to establish as the successor body to the OEEC, and in which both are represented as full members. The change of name from OEEC to OECD—dropping the word "European" and taking up the word "Development"—is highly significant. The creation of the OECD marks both the completion of European recovery and the recognition that what is now needed is economic cooperation and development on a much wider scale.

What, in practice, does this mean? I have already mentioned many of the problems that have to be faced. Some of them are highlighted by the creation of the European Community, some are thrown into sharper relief by the current negotiations with Great Britain. All of them, however, are likely to prove easier to solve now that the Community is a growing reality, and all of them demand political decisions within the "open partnership" which is now proposed. There is the problem of economic growth. The member countries of the OECD have set as their joint target a 50 percent increase in their gross national product for the decade 1960 to 1970. There is the problem of the business cycle; here too concerted efforts will be needed to ensure that expansion is steady. There is the problem of world currencies and world liquidity. Various solutions to this problem have been mooted, and influential voices in Europe have called for the creation of a European Reserve Fund which could greatly strengthen the currencies of the Community's member states and help bring greater stability to others. There is the problem of world agriculture. Here, the Community's common policy may prove to be a lever capable of setting in motion more effective concerted actions; and the Commonwealth problems posed by the prospect of British entry into the EEC could provide a real incentive for the establishment of world-wide arrangements similar, perhaps, to those recently proposed in the GATT. There is the vast and pressing problem of the developing countries. The OECD is already active in an attempt to coordinate and increase the volume of aid to these areas. Meanwhile, the Community is engaged in renegotiating the arrangements for association between it and the overseas countries, mostly in Africa, that have become independent since the EEC treaty was signed. This, and the British negotiation, may provide an opportunity for diversifying the various forms of aid already granted, and in particular for reducing the preferential aspect of the association by cutting the Community's external tariff on a number of tropical products. There is the further problem of the low-wage countries. Here again, some steps have been taken in the GATT to widen the market outlets of these countries without disrupting industry within the Community; and here again, the British negotiation provides a further stimulus for reviewing the whole problem. These are only some of the problems. I must not fail to add the crucial question of trade with the Communist bloc. Here, too, the application of a common commercial policy by the European Community should prove greatly to the free world's advantage—and all the more so if it can be coordinated with those of the Community's partners.

All these problems, of course, are much more than a matter of commercial policy, or even of foreign economic policy. For the Community, for the United States, for the whole free world, they are a matter of the utmost political importance. If we do not succeed in solving them, we shall risk exposing ourselves to that familiar reproach with which Communist ideology has always taunted free economic society—that it is weakened and may be destroyed by its own "internal contradictions." We may be sure that there is nothing that the Communist world would like better than to see the free world split asunder by its economic problems; to see both the European Community and the United States retreat once more into shortsighted policies of protectionism and isolationism at once inefficient and divisive; to see the economic growth of free nations dwarfed by Communist expansion or crippled by economic crises; to see their currencies shaken and their reserves depleted; to see farm surpluses endlessly accumulate while growing populations starve; to see low-wage manufactures either rot in the factories or ruin the industries of more highly developed countries; to see state-trading countries disrupt the free market; to see, in a word, the breakdown of our economic and political systems because we lack the wit, the courage, and the political will to face the challenges and opportunities that our age so abundantly provides.

I have painted a black picture. But I have done so only to suggest the penalties of failure. For myself, I cannot believe that we shall fail. We are already proving—and we must prove—that together we can control our destinies and build a better, happier, and more just world, a world in which, through strength and not through weakness, it may one day be possible to replace so-called "peaceful coexistence" with genuine and lasting peace.

At various points in these remarks I have had occasion to quote Alexis de Tocqueville. I should like to conclude as he himself concluded his study of *Democracy in America;* for his words are now more than ever relevant to my theme.

For myself, who now look back from this extreme limit of my task, and discover from afar, but at once, the various objects which have attracted my more attentive investigation upon my way, I am full of apprehensions and of hopes. I perceive mighty dangers which it is possible to ward off —mighty evils which may be avoided or alleviated; and I cling with a firmer hold to the belief, that for democratic nations to be virtuous and prosperous they require but to will it. I am aware that many of my contemporaries maintain that nations are never their own masters here below, and that they necessarily obey some insurmountable and unintelligent power, arising from anterior events, from their race, or from the soil and climate of their country. Such principles are false and cowardly; such principles can never produce aught but feeble men and pusillanimous nations. Providence has not created mankind entirely independent or entirely free. It is true that around every man a fatal circle is traced, beyond which he cannot pass; but within the wide verge of that circle he is powerful and free: as it is with man, so with communities. The nations of our time cannot prevent the conditions of men from becoming equal; but it depends upon themselves whether the principle of equality is to lead them to servitude or freedom, to knowledge or barbarism, to prosperity or to wretchedness.[23]

CHRONOLOGY
BIBLIOGRAPHY
NOTES
INDEX

CHRONOLOGY

1945
December 27   International Bank for Reconstruction and De-velopment and International Monetary Fund established.

1946
September 19   Winston Churchill, in a speech at Zurich University, urges the creation of "a kind of United States of Europe."

1947
June 5   General George Marshall proposes American aid to stimulate economic recovery in Europe.

October 29   Creation of Benelux, a customs and economic union of Belgium, the Netherlands, and Luxembourg.

1948
January 1   General Agreement on Tariffs and Trade (GATT) comes into force.

April 16   Signature of the Convention for European Economic Cooperation: the birth of the Organization for European Economic Cooperation (OEEC).

1949
May 5   Signature of the Statute of the Council of Europe.

1950

May 9   Robert Schuman, French Foreign Minister, makes his historic declaration proposing that French and German coal and steel be pooled under common institutions open to the other countries of Europe.

1951

April 18   The treaty setting up the European Coal and Steel Community (ECSC) is signed in Paris.

1952

May 27   The European Defense Community (EDC) treaty is signed in Paris.

August 10   The ECSC High Authority starts work in Luxembourg.

September 10   The ECSC Common Assembly holds its first session in Strasbourg.

1953

February 10   The ECSC's "common market" for coal, iron ore, and scrap is opened.

May 1   The ECSC's "common market" for steel is opened.

1954

August 1   The ECSC's "common market" for special steels is opened.

August 30   The EDC treaty fails.

December 21   An Agreement of Association between the United Kingdom and the ECSC is signed in London.

1955

June 1–3   At a Conference in Messina, the Foreign Ministers of the six ECSC member states propose further measures of European integration.

1956

May 7   Consultation Agreement between Switzerland and the ECSC is signed.

1957

March 25   The treaties setting up the European Economic Community (EEC) and the European Atomic Energy Community (Euratom) are signed in Rome.

1958

January 1   The Rome treaties come into force.

February 9   The ECSC's five-year transition period comes to an end.

March 19–21   The European Parliament holds its first session in Strasbourg.

November 8   Cooperation Agreement between the United States and Euratom is signed.

1959

January 1   First internal tariff cuts and quota liberalization measures are effected in the EEC. A common market for nuclear materials is established by Euratom.

February 4   Cooperation Agreement between the United Kingdom and Euratom is signed.

June 8   Greece applies for association with the EEC.

July 31   Turkey applies for association with the EEC.

October 6   Cooperation Agreement between Canada and Euratom is signed.

November 20   Convention for European Free Trade Association signed by Austria, Denmark, Norway, Portugal, Sweden, Switzerland, and the United Kingdom.

1960

May 12   EEC decides to accelerate implementation of the Rome Treaty.

1961

July 9   Agreement of Association between Greece and the EEC is signed in Athens.

July 18　Six Community countries issue Bonn Declaration in favor of political union.

August 1　The Republic of Ireland applies for membership of the EEC.

August 10　Denmark and the United Kingdom apply for membership of the EEC.

December 15　Austria, Sweden, and Switzerland request to open negotiations with the EEC.

1962

February 9　Spain applies for association with the EEC.

March 2　The United Kingdom applies for membership of the ECSC.

March 5　The United Kingdom applies for membership of Euratom.

March 7　Signature of Agreement in GATT between the United States and the EEC providing for substantial mutual tariff cuts.

April 30　Norway requests negotiations for membership of the EEC.

May 15　EEC decides on second acceleration of implementation of the Rome Treaty.

June 4　Portugal requests to open negotiations with the EEC.

BIBLIOGRAPHY

BIBLIOGRAPHICAL

European Community Information Service, Washington. *A Selected Bibliography on European Integration*. Washington, March 1961.

Services des Publications des Communautés Européennes. *Publications de la CEE*. Brussels, annual.

GENERAL

Ball, M. Margaret. *NATO and the European Union Movement*. New York, 1959.

Beever, R. Colin. *European Unity and the Trade Union Movements*. Leyden, 1961.

Beloff, Max. *Europe and the Europeans: An International Discussion*. London, 1957.

Council of Europe. *Handbook of European Organizations*. Strasbourg, 1956.

Dewhurst, J. Frederic, and others. *Europe's Needs and Resources*. New York, 1961.

Haines, C. Grove (ed.). *European Integration*. Baltimore, 1957.

Hartog, F. *European Trade Cycle Policy*. Leyden, 1959.

Haviland, H. Field, Jr. (ed.). *The United States and the Western Community*. Haverford, Pennsylvania, 1957.

Henderson, W. O. *The Zollverein*. Cambridge, 1939.

Jennings, W. Ivor. *A Federation of Western Europe*. London, 1940.

Lindsay, Kenneth. *European Assemblies*. New York, 1960.

List, F. *The National Systems of Political Economy*. Trans. S. S. Lloyd. London, 1916.

Macmahon, Arthur W. (ed.). *Federalism, Mature and Emergent*. New York, 1955.

Mayne, Richard. *The Community of Europe*. London, 1962.

Meade, James E. *Problems of Economic Union*. London, 1953.

Moore, Ben. *NATO and the Future of Europe*. New York, 1958.

National Industrial Conference Board. *Economic Unity in Europe*. New York, 1960.

Naumann, F. *Mitteleuropa*. Berlin, 1915.

Northrop, F. S. C. *European Union and United States Foreign Policy*. New York, 1954.

Political and Economic Planning. *European Organizations*. London, 1959.

Robertson, A. H. *European Institutions*. New York, 1959.

Sannwald, Rolf, and Jacques Stohler. *Wirtschaftliche Integration*. Basel and Tübingen, 1958.

Scitovsky, Tibor. *Economic Theory and Western European Integration*. London, 1958.

Tocqueville, Alexis de. *Democracy in America* (trans. Henry Reeve). Oxford, 1947.

Trempont, Jacques. *L'Unification de l'Europe*. Amiens and Brussels, 1955.

Triffin, Robert. *Europe and the Money Muddle*. New Haven, Conn., 1957.

United Nations. *Customs Unions: A League of Nations Contribution to the Study of Customs Union Problems*. New York, 1947.

United States Government Printing Office. *Foreign Economic Policy for the 1960's: Report of the Joint Economic Committee to the Congress of the United States*. Washington, 1962.

Viner, Jacob. *The Customs Union Issue*. New York and London, 1950.

—————— *International Economics*. Glencoe, Ill., 1951.

Zurcher, Arnold J. *The Struggle to Unite Europe, 1940–1958*. New York, 1958.

THE EUROPEAN COMMUNITIES

Allen, James Jay. *The European Common Market and the GATT*. Washington, 1960.

Beever, R. Colin. *Trade Unions and the Common Market*. Political and Economic Planning. London, 1962.

Beloff, Max. *New Dimensions in Foreign Policy*. London, 1961.

Benoit, Emile. *Europe at Sixes and Sevens*. New York, 1961.

Business International. *Europe's Mass Markets.* New York, 1960.

Cabot, Thomas D. *Common Market: Economic Foundation for a United States of Europe?* New York, 1959.

Campbell, A., and D. Thompson. *Common Market Law.* London, 1962.

Camps, Miriam. *Division in Europe.* Political and Economic Planning Occasional Paper No. 8. London, 1960.

—— *The European Common Market and American Policy.* Princeton, 1956.

—— *The European Common Market and Free Trade Area: A Progress Report.* Princeton, 1957.

—— *The European Free Trade Association: A Preliminary Appraisal.* Political and Economic Planning Occasional Paper No. 4. London, 1959.

—— *The First Year of the European Economic Community.* Princeton, 1958.

—— *Four Approaches to the European Problem.* Political and Economic Planning Occasional Paper No. 12. London, 1961.

—— *The Free Trade Area Negotiations.* Political and Economic Planning Occasional Paper No. 2. London, 1959.

Deniau, J. F. *The Common Market.* London, 1960. 2nd ed., 1961; 3rd ed., 1962.

Diebold, William, Jr. *The Schuman Plan.* New York, 1959.

Economist Intelligence Unit. *Britain and Europe.* London, 1957.

—— *The Commonwealth and Europe.* London, 1960.

Everett, Robinson O. (ed.) *European Regional Communities.* Duke University, N.C., 1962.

Federal Bar Association. *Institute on Legal Aspects of the European Community.* Washington, 1960.

Frank, Isaiah. *The European Common Market: An Analysis of Commercial Policy.* New York, 1961.

Haas, Ernst B. *The Uniting of Europe.* Stanford, California, 1958.

Hallstein, Walter. "Economic Integration and Political Unity in Europe." Lecture given before a joint meeting of Harvard University and the Massachusetts Institute of Technology, May 22, 1961. *Community Topics,* No. 2. London, 1961.

—— "Economic integration—an example of the association of states." Paper read to the XLth Congress of the International Law Association, Hamburg, August 8, 1960. *Report of the XLth Congress of the International Law Association*, pp. 13–32. London, 1961.

———— "Economic Integration as a Factor of Political Unification." Translated and reprinted from "Wirtschaftliche Integration als Faktor politischer Einigung," in *Wirtschaft, Gesellschaft und Kultur, Festgabe für Alfred Müller-Armack,* Herausgegeben von Franz Greiss und Fritz W. Meyer (Berlin, 1961), 267–278. Brussels, 1961.

———— Statement to the European Parliament at Strasbourg, March 20, 1958. Translated and reprinted. Brussels, 1958.

Heiser, H. J. *British Policy with Regard to the Unification Efforts on the European Continent.* Leyden, 1959.

Kitzinger, U. W. *The Challenge of the Common Market.* Oxford, 1961.

Knorr, Klaus E. *Euratom and American Policy.* Princeton, 1956.

Krassa, Lucie G. *The European Economic Community.* Maryland, 1959.

Legal Problems of the E.E.C. and the E.F.T.A. Report of a conference held in London in September 1960. London, 1961.

Lister, Louis. *Europe's Coal and Steel Community.* New York, 1960.

Marting, Elizabeth (ed.). *The European Common Market: New Frontier for American Business.* New York, 1958.

Mason, Henry L. *The European Coal and Steel Community.* The Hague, 1955.

Meyer, F. V. *The Seven.* London, 1960.

Monnet, Jean. *Les Etats-Unis d'Europe ont Commencé.* Paris, 1955.

Moore, Ben T. *Euratom: the American Interest in the European Atomic Energy Community.* New York, 1958.

Nutting, Anthony. *Europe Will Not Wait.* London, 1960.

Pinder, John. *Britain and the Common Market.* London, 1961.

Piquet, Howard S. *The European Free Trade Association: Implications for U.S. Exports.* New York, 1960.

Political and Economic Planning. *Agricultural Policy in the European Economic Community.* Occasional Paper No. 1. London, 1958.

———— *Agriculture, the Commonwealth, and the E.E.C.* Occasional Paper No. 14. London, 1961.

———— *Budgetary Control in the European Economic Community.* Occasional Paper No. 6. London, 1960.

—————— *Commonwealth Preference in the United Kingdom.* London, 1960.

—————— *Direct Elections and the European Parliament.* Occasional Paper No. 10. London, 1960.

—————— *Food Prices and the Common Market.* Occasional Paper No. 13. London, 1961.

—————— *France and the European Community.* Occasional Paper No. 11. London, 1961.

—————— *International Money and Capital Movements in Europe.* London, 1961.

—————— *Problems of Freer Trade in Europe.* London, 1958.

—————— *Proposals for a Common Agricultural Policy in E.E.C.* Occasional Paper No. 5. London, 1960.

—————— *Tariffs and Trade in Western Europe.* London, 1959.

—————— *Trade Diversion in Western Europe.* Occasional Paper No. 9. London, 1960.

Robertson, B. C. *Regional Development in the European Economic Community.* London, 1962.

Root, Franklin R. *The European Coal and Steel Community.* College Park, Maryland, 1955–56.

Stein, Eric, and Thomas L. Nicholson. *American Enterprise in the European Common Market: a Legal Profile.* Ann Arbor, Michigan, 1960.

Valentine, Donald G. *The Court of Justice and the European Coal and Steel Community.* The Hague, 1954.

Worswick, G. D. N. (ed.) *The Free Trade Area Proposals.* Oxford, 1960.

NOTES

1. Alexis de Tocqueville, *Democracy in America*, trans. by Henry Reeve, Oxford University Press, 1947, p. 285.

2. Ibid., pp. 286–287.

3. Ibid., p. 15.

4. Ibid., pp. 101–102.

5. Ibid., p. 102.

6. Ibid., p. 425.

7. J. Trempont, *L'Unification de l'Europe*, Amiens–Brussels, 1955, pp. 20–28; R. Sannwald and J. Stohler, *Wirtschaftliche Integration*, Basel–Tübingen, 1958, p. 8. The gross national product comparison is at 1954 prices and in real purchasing power; at official parity the contrast is even greater.

8. Tocqueville, p. 108.

9. J. E. Meade, *Problems of Economic Union*, London, 1953, pp. 9–10.

10. Cf. J.-F. Deniau, *The Common Market*, 2nd ed., London, 1961, pp. 11–17.

11. F. List, *The National System of Political Economy*, trans. by S. S. Lloyd, London, 1916, p. 93.

12. J. Viner, *International Economics*, Glencoe, Ill., 1951, p. 16.

13. J. Viner, *The Customs Union Issue*, New York–London, 1950, p. 41.

14. F. Naumann, *Mitteleuropa*, Berlin, 1915, p. 249.

15. W. O. Henderson, *The Zollverein*, Cambridge, 1939, p. 343.

16. *Customs Unions: A League of Nations Contribution to the Study of Customs Union Problems*, New York, 1947, p. 47.

17. Meade, *Problems of Economic Union*, p. 82.

18. Tocqueville, p. 5.

19. Tocqueville, p. 7.

20. Meade, *Problems of Economic Union*, p. 83.

21. James Jay Allen, *The European Common Market and the GATT*, Washington, D.C., 1960.

22. *Foreign Economic Policy for the 1960's: Report of the Joint Economic Committee to the Congress of the United States* (U.S. Government Printing Office, Washington, D.C., 1962), p. 8.

23. Tocqueville, pp. 598–599.

INDEX